ACQUIRED
Now What?

Embrace the flux and uncertainty of M&A and become
a savvy and bulletproof business professional

YOUR JOURNEY AWAITS!

Vigilant Press, LLC
P.O. Box 5365
Cary, NC 27512

Ordering Information
Currently available on Amazon and Kindle
Quantity Sales: Special discounts are available on quantity purchase by corporations, associations, and others.

Printed in the United States of America

Cover Design: Vigilant Press, LLC
Book Layout & Design: Vigilant Press, LLC
Series Editor: Jon Obermeyer, Venture Communications
Nights & Weekends Enabler: Coffee & Electronic Music

Library of Congress Cataloging-in-Publication Data
ISBN-13: 978-0692143384

First Edition

DEDICATION

To my beautiful wife, Courtney, and amazing daughter, Juliette, for their continued love and support to make me better each day.

To my late Grandfather, William Hull, for his many years of shared wisdom and laughter.

To my mother and sister for being fantastic co-pilots on our many adventures through life.

And thanks to each of you reading this right now and taking yourself forward.

Godspeed!

TAKE A DEEP BREATH

TABLE OF CONTENTS

INTRODUCTION: MY 16 REASONS FOR WRITING THIS BOOK

"No matter what people tell you, words and ideas can change the world."
—Robin Williams

Wait. . . the author of this book is a technologist, entrepreneur, and artist? No Ivy League MBA? No finance or Wall Street pedigree? What can he possibly teach me?

Mergers and acquisitions (M&A) is a generic business term that refers to the consolidation of companies or assets, where generally two companies are involved. M&A can include a number of different transactions, such as horizontal and vertical mergers, consolidations, tender offers, purchase of assets, and the recently popular talent-grab acquisitions called acqui-hires.

In many respects, M&A is like the institution of marriage, in which the consolidation of trust and love occurs between two unique and principled individuals. Mergers and acquisitions in business similarly lead to the consolidation of teams, processes, and philosophies. There are also transactions in marriage just as there are in M&A, such as transactions of love, support, undying faith, and the formation of a bond between two families.

If you've picked up this book, you're probably working for a company (or perhaps even own one) that's going through or will be going through M&A. Maybe you simply want to learn more about what this process entails, and what you can do to navigate it and come out on top. Maybe you've heard about the uncertainty M&A brings to a company and are concerned about what the future might hold for your career. Or maybe you're just trying to figure out how you're going to survive this upcoming storm.

Here's the good news . . . I'm here to help.

What's a person like me doing writing about M&A? Well, I've been through six acquisitions. Three of them have been small, whereas the rest have been of a much larger scope . . . and I'm only halfway through my career!

Like many of you reading this book right now, I am a lifelong learner and always looking to get better – both personally and professionally. So, as I looked around for sources on coping with or navigating the M&A process, I quickly realized that no one was writing about these concepts. At least, no one has written about them in a while, in a way that reflects the current state of M&A.

That's why I've written this book, to help you consciously cope with and navigate the M&A process and build the bulletproof professional career you want.

And if you aren't convinced that you need help with your journey through M&A yet, here are 16 reasons that illuminate the "why" behind my creation . . .

1. **M&A is here to stay.** If you follow business news, you know that it is as prevalent as ever. There are more than 14,000 M&A deals every year (the ones that are reported), and this affects roughly 10% of the U.S. workforce. Most other thriving countries globally share similar stats. So, if you work in a start-up or mid-sized company, or even a large public company, an acquisition is likely to occur in your impending future.

2. **This book is not your grandfather's M&A guide, from the days of horses and buggies.** Most M&A books were written a decade (or more) ago (can you believe it?). These books are so old that they have dust from the Y2K era on them. Some of these elderly M&A books talk about "combinations," which I think is the term that was used to refer to M&A back in 1901, when U.S. Steel bought Carnegie Steel for $5 billion. Several M&A books I unearthed appeared to have been composed on stone tablets—which not only makes them outdated and irrelevant, but also (surprise! surprise!) heavy. You should see their shipping charges on Amazon!

3. **Most M&A books are very dry and unfunny.** Despite all the chaos and trauma of an acquisition, there are some humorous interludes—many of which are unexpected. Humor is a great coping mechanism—a good laugh connects people instantly and lowers stress. So, I wanted to inject some of the stand-up *shticks* of Jerry Seinfeld and George Carlin into this sober topic. Tip your waitress, as I'm here all week. And don't forget to try the veal. . .

4. **My aim in this book is to be as pragmatic as possible.** This book looks at multiple acquisition scenarios, including both large and small deals, and provides a unique look at what happens during a "merger of equals" to give a realistic view of M&A. Please keep in mind that there are plenty of other deals that happen every day that won't be covered. Fear not, I'm planning on making this a series. Stay tuned!

5. **M&A is stoic and impersonal by nature.** It isn't supposed to be about the people. That's a bit raw and sobering to hear, but the harsh reality is that this is business, and it happens every day. In most cases, the potential buyers of your company have what I call a "Spreadsheet Mentality." They're looking at your name and your job as a row on a spreadsheet with your annual salary next to it, and there's no background consideration whatsoever. While

that isn't always the case, I want to help you move past that barrier and enable you to advocate for yourself and your direct reports when possible.

6. **I want to teach you how to be nimble and adaptable before, during, and after an acquisition.** You may need to redefine your role and figure out a new pathway, which means an acquisition can be an opportunity for your growth. Get excited!

7. **M&A could be the best thing that has happened to your career.** There's a lot of negative energy and uncertainty that surrounds the time before, during, and after an acquisition. Despite the uncertainties, I want you to be able to respond and adapt positively with the tools laid out in this book.

8. **This book builds on the personal development concepts** covered in the best-selling books *Emotional Intelligence* (Daniel Goleman), *Grit* (Angela Duckworth), and *Lean In* (Sheryl Sandberg). Onward.

9. **I want you to approach each day positively during an acquisition.** Through our unique "M&A Fitness Assessment ™,"I want you to know what it's like to have a "Green Light" status during an acquisition. You'll

gain pragmatic and positive alternatives to feelings of the 3P's (passivity, paralysis, and powerlessness). The positive approach you exhibit will also be contagious to those around you. As you figure out a path forward through the jungle, your peers and direct reports will want to follow you.

10. **You can play a leadership role during an acquisition.** Your job title may not change at all after reading this book. However, your initial, informal role in an acquisition might be that of a translator—such as one at the United Nations—interpreting the new company's culture so it is relevant to your old company. That way, everyone understands which standards, behaviors, and tools are essential, and which ones have become irrelevant.

11. **I want to help you hone your integration and innovation skills.** In your new leadership role (which might be ad hoc and informal), I want to help you increase skills that are highly valuable to your acquirer, especially if they aren't evident from a spreadsheet.

12. **I want to help you navigate trickier situations.** If you run into the "Yellow Light" and "Red Light" scenarios in the assessment tools, your odds of survival might not be so great. Let's work to answer the question: What to do then?

13. **When things are still in flux, it's the best time to make a bold move or two.** Regardless of where you are placed in the organizational hierarchy, this may be your moment. **Seize it!**

14. **I want to help you prepare for the possibility** of getting offered a relocation package or severance package.

15. **I want to enable you to determine when it's finally time to move on**. Stop wasting energy on a "no-win" situation. Why bloody your nose over and over again? It is your time, my friend!

16. **You need to be ready for the future.** Given the prevalence of M&A, I want to teach you how to be prepared for the next acquisition your company might undergo. It might be right around the corner! Wait for it...

I hope you find my contribution inspiring and helpful.

Keno Vigil

1

THE M&A SUPERSTORM: HOW COMMON IS IT?

> "Why join the navy if you can be a pirate?"
> — Steve Jobs

M&A is the new thing many folks in the business world are going gaga over, and it looks like this emerging trend will continue and perhaps even increase in the coming years.

Unfortunately, there is no official M&A source of statistics, such as the Bureau of Labor Statistics for the unemployment rate or the Centers for Disease Control and Prevention for flu virus outbreaks. However, such a source should exist. *Can I get an Amen?*

Because it doesn't, I can only tell you my story of experiencing six acquisitions in 20 years and give you an idea of the number of companies involved in M&A each year. M&A activity is steady—if not growing. It's definitely not on the decline.

Bring your shovel . . . M&A statistics are like an archaeological dig

An ancient M&A statistic (from 1989) estimates that "10 percent of the current U.S. workforce is involved in either a merger, acquisition, or related spinoff."[1]

If you extrapolate from the outdated statistic above, the chances remain high that YOU will be involved and caught up in an M&A transaction once in a decade, and possibly four times in a typical career spanning 40 years.

Whoa!

If you work for a start-up or your employer's business is currently being purchased, gutted, and prepared for a quick "flip," you might realize that even the once-per-decade statistic is inaccurate. Acquired companies tend to be acquired again. Isn't that as incontestable as one of Newton's laws?

If you've never been through an acquisition in your career and believe that the data doesn't lie, allow me to paint the clear picture—one that will prove an acquisition will happen to you eventually. Let's get you ready!

Take a moment and look at M&A from a global perspective. The global M&A value reached a record $1.2 trillion in the first quarter of 2018. This dollar value

---

[1] Buono, Anthony F., Bowditch, James L., *The Human Side of Mergers & Acquisitions*, BeardBooks, 1989

was an increase of 60 percent, whereas the number of deals decreased by 11 percent when compared with the first quarter of 2017. Therefore, this has been the strongest first quarter since records started to be documented in 1980.

Okay, so, how prevalent is M&A in the United States?

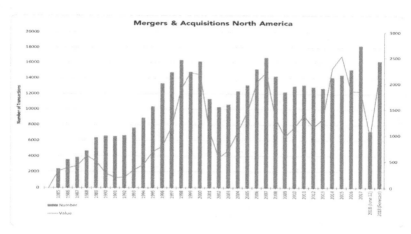

Figure 1: IMAA: M&A in North America

The Institute for Mergers, Acquisitions and Alliances (IMAA) reported a record 15,010 deals made in 2017 in the United States, which was a 12.2 percent increase over the number of deals struck in 2016. In addition, the deal value increased by 59 percent, and the number of deals decreased by 11 percent in comparison with the first quarter of 2017. M&A in the U.S. accounted for 47 percent of all deal activity.[2]

If you find this eye-opening, you will be amazed by the next section for sure!

[2] IMAA

2

MORE ~~MURDERS & EXECUTIONS~~ ON THE WAY ;-)

"Just cause you got the monkey off your back doesn't mean the circus has left town."
—George Carlin

Robust M&A activity is expected to continue as U.S. tax reform and economic growth in Europe drive business deals. A total of 49 percent of the dealmakers predict an increase of up to 25 percent in M&A activity for 2018. Their top three M&A objectives are as follows: acquiring undervalued assets, acquiring high-growth businesses, and cutting costs through economies of scale.

If you follow general business news like me, you probably read a notable M&A story weekly. It seems like I get emails from Crunchbase and similar sources daily, detailing the latest Silicon Valley acquisitions at mouth-dropping valuations. Moreover, the deals seem to be getting bigger and bigger. There is clearly a lot of cash out there.

The biggest deal by far was the AOL–Time Warner merger in 2000 at $164 billion, which ultimately turned out to be a flop and resulted in a split between the two companies in 2009.

Dell Inc. and EMC also came together in a $66 billion deal, forming the world's largest privately-controlled tech company. And, most recently, a colorful merger of yellow and pink was formed with Sprint and T-Mobile, making their collaboration official.

Ready for a round of beer?

Well, in 2016, Anheuser-Busch InBev SA bought rival SABMiller plc for $104 billion in principle. According to Yahoo Finance, that deal represented the largest ever merger in the beer industry. Other notable deals include:

- Cigna–Express Scripts (2018) ($69 billion)
- Keurig–Dr Pepper (2018) ($18.7 billion)
- Amazon–Whole Foods (2017) ($13.7 billion)
- Walt Disney–21st Century Fox (2017) ($68 billion)
- Exxon–Mobil (1999) ($78 billion)

Last, but not least—and probably the most controversial and drawn out deal recently—is the AT&T and Time Warner merger for $85 billion that has struggled to get approval. However, at the time of the editing of this book, it has just gained approval to proceed.

What about the deals you don't hear about?

Many deals, especially among small LLCs and S corporations, happen below the radar—especially the sale of small entities to new owners, as it happened with the print shop I worked at in my early twenties. You will learn more about that adventure shortly, so fasten your seatbelts!

For now, check out the figure below.

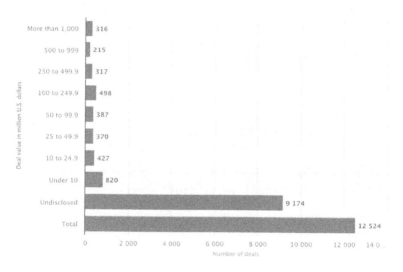

Figure 2: United States Deal Value in Millions [3]

Not only are the majority of the known deals from smaller companies whose acquisition is worth less than 10 million dollars, but thousands of other deals are undisclosed.

That means deals are happening all over the place, in

[3] https://www.statista.com/statistics/245977/number-of-munda-deals-in-the-united-states/

companies large and small, right under our noses.

And it's showing no sign of stopping. A 2017 survey by the consulting firm Deloitte found that the respondents were optimistic the number of M&A deals would increase in 2018. In addition, almost two-thirds of corporate respondents and three-quarters of private equity respondents predicted an upturn in transaction volume.[4]

The larger the company, the greater its pace of anticipated deal flow. A total of 35 percent of large corporations and 22 percent of small companies express that they expect to acquire businesses in the future.

In the words of Barney Stinson from the hit TV show *How I Met Your Mother*: "It's gonna be LEGEND... wait for it... and I hope you're not lactose intolerant because the second half of that word is DAIRY. "

---

[4] Deloitte 2018 M&A Trends Report

3

TALENT GRAB: THE RISE OF THE ACQUIHIRE

"Finding good players is easy. Getting them to play as a team is another story."
—Casey Stengel

So, we know that M&A is more than prevalent in the U.S., and that it's not slowing down in the coming years. But the real question is as follows:

Why are these companies acquiring with such enthusiasm?

The majority are looking forward to acquiring new technology or building out a digital strategy. Some are looking for transformational deals, whereas others are seeking smaller strategic acquisitions. And others are just looking to grow through acquisition.

According to the report by Deloitte, technology acquisition is the number one driver of M&A pursuits.[5] This includes staying ahead of expanding customer

---

[5] Deloitte, Ibid.

bases in existing markets or adding to products or services. Talent acquisition (also known as an acqui-hire) is an increasingly popular motivator for M&A activity as well.

According to CBI Insights[6], acqui-hire is a relatively recent phenomenon. Instead of buying companies for their products or even making a potential financial contribution, acquirers are buying teams of smart people (generally, engineers) who have a history of working well together, hoping that the integration of these teams might accelerate and advance their businesses.

The acqui-hire offers a nice alternative to death—a soft landing, if you prefer—for start-ups that are not successful (or not successful enough) and those that may be hitting the "Series A Crunch." It allows the acquired companies' investors to recoup some or all of their money and might give founders/the team a bit of money, a job, and options/bonuses with the help of the acquirer.

Another rationale behind M&A is plain arrogance on the part of acquirers or, in more diplomatic terms, the philosophy that "we acquire because we can." It sounds brash, but when you have a hungry board and plenty of cash in the bank, it is a reality.

Large companies hoard large amounts of cash on their balance sheets. For example, SPGlobal.com

[6] https://www.cbinsights.com/research/

reported in 2016 that among the roughly 2,000 U.S. non-financial corporate borrowers, the top 1 percent (~25 companies) held more than half the record— that is, $1.9 trillion in total cash and short- and long-term liquid investments in the U.S.[7] That's a lot of purchasing power!

Activist investors, and the Street (Wall Street) in general are always clamoring for high returns, and there's nothing like a pending deal to distract them. However, some of it is timeline-driven, based on previously-raised funds.

Believe it or not, the importance of shareholder value applies across the board. A study conducted by Transaction Advisors, which covered 20 years of M&A activity (and included 25,082 firms), found that firms underperform in the market when they are inactive in terms of announcing acquisitions or divestments. Firms outperform the market the more frequently they announce acquisitions. Likewise, younger firms only outperform the market during their first three years as public companies when they announce very high acquisition frequency, thereby signaling growth.

Transaction Advisors' study also found a causality link between firms' past performance and future frequency of M&A activity, and between the frequency of M&A activity and future performance.[8] This offers a possible explanation for the cyclical nature of M&A.

---

[7] https://www.spglobal.com/our-insights/
[8] https://www.transactionadvisors.com/insights/2016-srs-acquiom-ma-deal

Overall, firms achieve superior total shareholder returns with an M&A portfolio management program, which includes undertaking several acquisitions per year on average.

In addition to technological, talent, and purchasing pursuits, along with shareholder value, there's also **FOMO** (Fear of Missing Out) at work here. For example, you might say that if someone is a part of Verizon, T-Mobile, or Vodafone, and they just watched AT&T snap up Time Warner, their options have just narrowed considerably.

And let's not forget divestitures, which is another source of corporate flux and churn. According to Deloitte, 70 percent of corporate and private equity respondents say that they plan to sell units or assets in 2018—an increase of 48 percent since the spring of 2016.[9] Respondents cite a change in strategy as their main reason to divest businesses. Corporations with gross revenue of over $1 billion expect an unsolicited bid to be placed for one of their non-core business units by more than a two-to-one margin, as compared with the expectations for the same in smaller companies.

Having looked at all this data and simply perceiving what's going on around me, I can tell you for certain that M&A isn't going away. However, I don't recall taking a class in college that covered how to navigate one of these when it happens. I'm sure I'm not alone.

[9] Deloitte, Ibid.

But maybe, together, we can change that. . .

For those of you whose eyes are a bit glazed over by the barrage of bar charts and statistics, fear not! I felt that providing context was important to better define the landscape. Now that we have accomplished just that, we are going to get into the pragmatic and actionable things you can do as you navigate your next acquisition.

Ready? I'm excited to share my war stories with you!

4

PINBALL WIZARD: PLAYING—AND WINNING—THE M&A GAME

"Nobody trusts anyone, or why did they put tilt on a pinball machine..."
—Steve McQueen

A few years ago, my fiancé (now my wife) got me a 1970s pinball machine.

Let me give you some context. When I was growing up in New Jersey, we had a Star Trek pinball machine from the early 80s in our basement. I played with it until its analog parts needed to be replaced. My wife recalled the conversations I had with her about those nostalgic moments of my childhood and seized the opportunity when it presented itself. She gifted me a 1976 Bally Hang Glider, and it occupies a place of honor in our semi-formal dining room.

Yep, that's right. In a place where most people show off the buffet table filled with their heirloom china, we have the Hang Glider. After all, our pinball machine is an antique in its own right, built when Jimmy Carter was President and Jobs and Woz were in the garage developing the Apple computer.

Don't get me wrong—we have more computers in the house than we can possibly use, and own an HTC Vive, the latest camera gear, gaming consoles, and a semi-automated smart home powered by open-source software. Alexa can control all our lights and even lock the doors and close the garage on a schedule. Feel free to ask me about Bitcoin or the top 25 crypto-blockchain start-ups, the Internet of Things, the latest software development framework, singularity, and most things associated with Ray Kurzweil.

However, I see value in old things—and this is especially true for this 40-year-old pinball machine. You just can't replicate the feeling you get when banging around on that huge machine with its flashing lights and whirring music of ringtone dings. A pinball machine is very retro on the reboot. Whenever you want to play a new round, you have to feed it quarters. You can open it up and bear witness to a large collection of multi-colored wires and switches—it is fascinating! Today's machines are driven by a small computer and have minimal moving parts, if any. On the other hand, mine has 30 years of dust, countless moving parts, and miles of colored wires.

Pinball takes me back to another era—an era of going out with your friends to an arcade. Pinball was gaming before there was "gaming." It has an interesting history of innovation and technological breakthroughs. In this respect, while conducting research for this book, I discovered some of the following interesting facts:

- Pinball was banned from the early 1940s to the mid-1970s in most of America's prominent cities, including New York City, Los Angeles, and Chicago. Many lawmakers during that time believed pinball to be a mafia-run racket and a time- and dime-waster for the impressionable youth.[10] Isn't it interesting how we are currently having a similar debate with respect to certain console games?
- NYPD once made Prohibition-style raids on pinball. Sounds crazy, right?
- In 1976, the New York City pinball ban was overturned. So, my machine was likely one of the first off the line.

Our Hang Glider pinball machine is so vintage that it doesn't record the high scores. Wondering why? Well, it is because the analog number wheels can only display five digits. You can't save your username and high score at the end of a killer session. We have to write them down (old-school style) on a legal pad to keep a record for bragging rights.

So, Keno, what the heck does this have to do with M&A?

---

[10] https://www.popularmechanics.com/technology/g284/4328211-new/

The M&A game, like pinball machines, has survived into the modern era. And even with the rise of technology and the information age, the game still has the same objective. You want to win, period. And there are ways you can make sure you do.

It isn't easy. Playing a pinball game is a stand-up experience. You balance and lean in. You can't just slam the buttons. With all the intuition of a Pinball Wizard, you have to feel your way toward the high score.

The popper or plunger is the part of a pinball device that launches the ball vertically into the raised playfield. You control when you want to put the silver ball into play. You don't want to start the game without being prepared. For pinball, this means being ready and focused to begin. For M&A, this means having that same competitive drive and getting all your resources behind you. Without preparation and a desire to succeed, you're not in the game.

Once the game starts, you want to keep the silver ball in play for as long as possible. Not only do you want to keep it in constant contact with the pinball flippers, but you don't want to let go of the controls for even a second and lose it. When translated into the business world, this tells you to always be "in touch" with your customers and team members. You also want to stay playing as long as possible and not hand over the controls to your rival.

The "drain" is the dead zone located below the flippers, through which your ball exits and returns to the popper. You should do whatever you can to avoid the drain and stay in the game. Allow the secondary flippers to help you. There are allies out there who will also keep the game going and increase your score. For example, mentors are often instrumental to your success.

However, don't overdo it. Avoid the "Tilt" and "Slam Tilt" factors that void your play. Pinball rewards subtlety and a soft touch, and penalizes those who attempt to strong-arm the game to force the achievement of a higher score. This reminds you not to come on too strong and overwhelm anyone with whom you're talking when building professional relationships.

And never forget: My "heavy metal" pinball machine isn't going anywhere. It's a fully analog beast—solid and built to last. Sure, I might have to replace levers and re-solder some wires from time to time. However, that's part of the authentic experience of playing the game and overall journey. "Game Over" isn't included in my personal or professional plans. And it shouldn't be in yours either . . . **You got this!**

5

THE CHAMELEON GENE:
VERSATILITY BUSINESS TRAITS

"The art of life lies in a constant readjustment to our surroundings."
— Okakura Kakuzō

Winning the M&A game also means you need to stay on your toes. Surviving an acquisition is all about adapting and improvising in new environments and dealing with ambiguity, mixed messages, and uncertainty.

Exhibiting resilience and adapting come easily to me today. However, that wasn't always the case. Throughout my childhood, just like many of you, I was presented with numerous challenging situations that evolved these traits.

I was born in Las Vegas, New Mexico, and lived with my parents in nearby Santa Fe. I know what you're thinking right now—there's a Las Vegas in New Mexico? Yes— a somewhat sleepy, couple of stoplights kind of place. No Trip Advisor or Yelp reviews there.

Ok, so my father's heritage was a mix of Spanish and American Indian, whereas my mother was Irish and German. My dad was an artist and a restaurateur, and although my mom was a classic hippie and free spirit, she was an exceptionally loving and smart woman.

Living in New Mexico was an interesting time for all of us. We lived in an underground adobe house that had sunken into the landscape. And yes—I'm talking about real adobe walls, no air conditioning, and a full grass roof you could play on and needed to mow. Both of my parents were connected to the local arts community and tended to look at things quite differently. In fact, my mother casually knew the famous painter Georgia O'Keeffe, who lived nearby in her later years. Her compound was slightly more modern and plush than our below-grade living quarters.

Unfortunately, just before my fifth birthday, my parents split up. We moved across the country to Parsippany, NJ, where my mother had grown up, and her parents still lived. As you can imagine, moving from the desert in the southwest to northern New Jersey was quite the culture shock for me. Living in a normal house above ground was a new experience too; however, the grass still needed to be mowed. (Ha!).

Years later, my mom initiated shift #2—our first family merger—when she remarried. Bob, my new stepfather, owned a tennis club with his father and came from a very respected Italian Catholic family.

We were quickly submerged into a unique subculture of large Italian families in the northeast. I became an altar boy at St. Peter's church and a semi-devout follower of the New York Yankees and New York Giants. I was also a tenacious collector of baseball cards. I would spend every cent I earned on the constant pursuit to open a pack with that new rookie card. However, much like most of the other card-collecting dreamers, my packs were a bust nine out of ten times.

All seemed to be going very well for us—that is, until my stepfather, Bob, was stricken with lung cancer. Cancer spread to his kidneys and, eventually, to his brain. Despite countless treatments and operations, his cancer took hold and delivered the final blow within a year. We were all devastated, as you can imagine. However, as crazy as it sounds, my mother, sister, and I became estranged from the larger Italian family shortly after my stepfather passed away. A very bizarre situation for anyone, but those were the cards dealt. It became clear to us that it was time for our next chapter. Ciao, ciao, ciao.

So, after this tragic event, my mother moved us to the south so we could be closer to her parents, who were retired by then. With my sister, Vanessa, and cat, Calvin, in tow, we were southbound to a small and charming town on the coast of North Carolina, known as Morehead City.

Just like our previous trek across the country, this was

yet another culture shock for us. One of my most vivid initial memories is that of meeting our neighbors. Picture this—I was proudly sporting my clean high-top white Nikes, whereas everyone around me was wearing distressed leather rainbow flip-flops or low top soccer trainers. *Think "Members Only" jacket meets {insert surfing company brand} hoodie.*

Obviously, it didn't end with just the clothing. I had enough shiny gel in my spiked hair to make a porcupine jealous, even though the popular hairstyle of the time was straight long hair below the ear. The presence of hair products for guys was unheard of— that is, of course, unless you'd moved from New Jersey. Yep, I was the strange one. Laugh all you want, but even I can't fail to admit that the situation was too funny!

Soon after getting settled in, my mother became a real estate agent and, shortly after that, a house flipper. This meant we moved a lot, vacating our house soon after it was fixed up and ready to sell. It is crazy when I think about it now, but my mother would spend all that time and money on upgrades to get the home just how she liked it only to list it for sale. On a few occasions, we opted to rent the property instead of undergoing the quick flip.

As the "man" of the house, I learned a great deal about home remodeling from various contractors at a young age. This experience, in turn, proved to be extremely useful when I purchased my first home years later. My mother's house-flipping skills were honed way before anyone decided to create a cable television show about it. This wasn't the typical line of work on which a single mother in the south embarked. Then again, my mother tended to march to the beat of her own drum.

Therefore, in that spirit, she flipped religions, abandoning our previous strict New Jersey Catholicism and her Sunday School class (CCD) for a surreal strain of Southern Pentecostal variation. This was marked by tent revivals with frenzied preachers in white suits healing and speaking in tongues. I might have stretched the truth a little bit here; however, that experience is certainly available if you want it. Although it was a strong and growing group that did a lot of good for the community, it certainly raised many questions from my sister and me. We tended to be a bit skeptical about anything that consumed our mother's attention.

First-world problems, right?

In retrospect, it wasn't all that bad, and I emerged from this New Mexico-New Jersey-North Carolina geographical arc of childhood remarkably intact. In fact, I was a polished stone from all the tumbles to which I'd been subjected. Because of my mother and her instincts, a different lens of the world was available to me. After all the varied situations with which we were presented, I possessed a refined skill of being able to encounter and interact with new challenges more comfortably. Today, I like to think that I can pick up on the social codes, protocols, and nuances of language and know how to respond effectively. Or, at least, I believe I can fake it well.

To be candid, I did fantasize about things being more structured and normal throughout my childhood. I often wished our mother could be our concierge chauffeur and pick us up from travels, sporting games, and events, or even something as silly as seeing her help out at school functions like other PTA moms. However, as I matured, I realized that 'normal' is overrated and boring— in addition to being relative for each family. I realized my mother bestowed on us a gift that I'm incredibly grateful to her for fostering. I'm not even sure whether she recognized what an impact she was making on my sister and me at the time. As the oldest of seven brothers and sisters, resourcefulness, resilience, and adaptation seemed to be ingrained in her DNA.

So, by the time I was ready to enter the workforce, I had taken my mother's skills to heart. I knew how to adapt, how to respond to new challenges—and being in a new environment had become second nature to me. Little did I know, my story wouldn't change all that much.

If anything, entering into work would put those abilities to the test.

6

UNO, DOS, TRES ACQUISITIONS

"Success is not final, failure is not fatal:
it is the courage to continue that counts."
—Winston Churchill

Was I born with a silver spoon in my mouth? Not so much. . .

I funded my way through college by undertaking many part-time gigs. However, two of the most long-lasting and notable ones were those in a local print shop as a designer/project manager (among many other roles) and at a popular downtown restaurant as a bartender on the weekends. The two jobs comprised two very different worlds. Both part-time gigs were incredibly rewarding, but for strikingly different reasons.

The restaurant business is a fast-paced environment and necessitates its employees put in long, back-breaking hours. It is a work-hard-play-hard environment. You have to remember that the smaller "mom-and-pop" places sprinkled throughout the U.S.

are ultimately all about the celebration of food and the people. In fact, I've traveled to many countries in Europe and southeast Asia and have experienced the same openness and warmth from those establishments as I have from the ones here. I warmly (and cheekily) referred to my co-workers at the time as "Restaurant Carnies." This was a term of endearment, as the group generally was a bunch of life-loving misfits from all over who enjoyed food and fun.

Hand-to-heart, I can confidently say that hospitality folks are some of the most genuine, shirt-off-their-backs kind of people with whom you will ever have the pleasure of interacting. Many of the relationships I formed as a part-time server and bartender are still going strong to this day, many years later. I have always said that everyone should have a stint working in the hospitality industry in their young adult life. You have to trust me on that one. . .

The print shop, on the other hand, operated at a relatively slower pace. It was a much more creative and dynamic professional environment, but it allowed me to don as many hats as I wanted. I would be taking sales orders and doing client visits one day, and then head down to the computer for hours the next. Speaking of hours, the business operated during standard 9-5 work hours. Obviously, this was very different from the nightlife atmosphere of a bustling restaurant and bar.

Small businesses are a fantastic testing ground to see how you will weather the start-up world on your own. The print shop was a fairly well-known brand at the time and, interestingly enough, it was sold three times during my short tenure. Aside from the personal family mergers during my childhood, this was my first professional, up-close and personal stint in experiencing how a company changes its owners.

Acquisition #1: The original owners—a couple in their mid-thirties with backgrounds in the mortgage and construction industry—had saved up and wanted to own a franchise. Despite not having any background in the design or printing industry, they jumped in feet first. They hacked along for about 11 months until the wife and co-owner became pregnant with their second child. They re-assessed their situation overall and opted to sell the business and return to their less-demanding and balanced corporate jobs.

Acquisition #2: They sold the business to a serial entrepreneur, who was also the owner of a family steakhouse chain in Iowa. Let's call him Mr. Steakhouse. He was a quiet and genuine guy, but he managed everything to the penny. Most memorably, he gave me a raise of 39 cents per hour. He was proud of his financial acumen even, but a bit surprised that I wasn't equally as impressed. This business was not high margin, and also was going through a slow time, so he thought he was doing as much as he could with the data he had. Mr. Steakhouse was a great guy and certainly taught me a thing or two about managing a business on a shoestring budget. Unfortunately, he was ultimately spread too thin, with his other endeavors stealing his focus. It was the classic case of a serial entrepreneur's business ADD (attention deficit disorder).

Acquisition #3: He put the company out on the block and it was shortly acquired by a couple from upstate New York who wanted something to manage and keep them busy before retirement. This New York power couple had owned a high-end marketing agency for years. So this line of work wasn't a stretch for them like it was for the previous owners. However, the jobs were much smaller in scope and, as with people with a creative streak, they tended to manage operations more on emotion and handshakes than spreadsheets. This was a welcome change that allowed us to undertake more creative work, although it also put us in a pickle or two when we went up against much larger printing/design firms. In the end, they secured some large contracts, and everything seemed to work out for them.

I, however, had learned all I could. I adapted, experienced company turmoil, and had learned how to work with a team and my ever-changing employers. It was time for me to move on.

Onward!

7

VENTURING OUT:
AIRWALK NETWORKS AND PPD

> "Do. Or do not. There is no try."
> —Yoda, Jedi Master

I've always been entrepreneurial, even when I was young. While many middle-class kids growing up in the U.S. have lemonade stands as their first business venture, I opted for jobs a bit on the fringe. I collected and sold baseball cards in my early years, then opted for freelance design work (CAD drawings) and physical labor renovation projects at my mother's rental houses when I got into high school.

So, I took this opportunity of leaving the little design and print shop to refocus my attention on turning my web consulting business, which I had kept alive in an only-do-jobs-that-interest-me kind of way, to a more serious business venture. As luck would have it, just as I was getting back into a full site redesign project for a new client, a fresh idea hit me and my good friend and roommate—let's call him Murray—and we just couldn't shake it.

To give you a bit more context, Murray was a savvy network engineer working at Nortel Networks, which was a bit of a troubled company at the time. There seemed to be weekly layoffs, and as you can imagine, these situations tend to breed many innovation-focused start-ups.

Our new venture was exciting for many reasons and had serious potential to scale quickly. Broadband and wireless technology was evolving and offered a large addressable market. Therefore I, along with my network engineering wizard of a roommate, launched and bootstrapped a WISP (Wireless Internet Service Provider) business, which we proudly named **Air Walk Networks**.

You have to remember that back then, Internet connections—especially broadband ones—were beyond expensive for most broke students living off campus. We aimed to change that by focusing on college apartment complexes as our main distribution sites. The complexes would purchase the main hub, and we would spread the bandwidth among the hundred, in some cases thousands, of apartments by leveraging our onsite hardware and strategically-placed amplified antennas.

Unfortunately, our "moons"—and by moons, I mean regulations—were not aligned with our vision. This entire market was undergoing changes, and we were certainly not the only WISP start-up affected.

Now, I'm convinced we could have pressed on if we had opted for angel funding and beyond. However, at the time, there were other forces at play and, sometimes, you just need to move on. But the experience was exciting and I had no regrets. My first failed start-up—CHECK!

After the glorious failure of my first bootstrapped venture, I decided to heal my wounds and jump into the life of corporate America for a bit. After a short consulting stint at SAS, an analytics juggernaut in Cary, NC, I went to work for PPD—a multi-billion-dollar NASDAQ-listed organization that specializes in clinical research.

At the time, there were approximately 10,000 employees spread globally. Now, let's be clear. I had never dreamed of working for a conservative pharmaceutical research organization, but growing up in northern New Jersey (a.k.a., Pharma Land), I had indeed considered it as a possible career option. Life is enriched by a diversity of experiences, so I figured why not?

During my tenure with PPD, I traversed the corporate ranks relatively quickly—going from a systems developer and business analyst to eventually running a small R&D team and reporting to the executive director of Enterprise Architecture.

You see, I love building digital products that solve business problems, talking to customers, giving executive presentations, and ultimately building highly effective (and happy) teams. So, this was a great time to be leading an R&D team, as it was rewarding both personally and professionally.

I also fostered a strong relationship and trust with many of the senior leadership team members—but most notably with our CIO, which certainly helped when I needed roadblocks removed for my R&D experimentation. Looking back, I would have to attribute this relatively quick ascension to the many relationships I nurtured throughout the ranks and across the departments. I was always willing to help and go the extra mile for team members, and they reciprocated my efforts in turn.

Being at the helm of PPD's first innovation R&D team, it was our mission to uncover the gems among ideas and experiment with their viability. We created Innovation Storm, an open innovation program that helped capture and prioritize ideas from the roughly 11,000 global employees in a fun and competitive way.

The platform essentially allowed everyone to vote (crowdsourced style) for a given idea, resulting in the best ideas bubbling to the top. Think of it as a leaderboard for company initiatives. I always said that you never knew where the good nuggets would come from, and that was illustrated time and again by the gems submitted by the entry-level employees and members of the senior ranks alike. **You had a serious voice even as an intern!**

In the drug development world, in which it generally takes 10 years and a BILLION dollars to create a drug, any meaningful innovation is welcomed with open arms. The industry at the time was very heavy on paper documentation, wet ink signatures, and dry physical storage for files. Such an environment was ripe for disruption.

One of our most notable projects was PPD PatientView, the industry's first online patient portal designed to increase the engagement and retention of participants in clinical trials.

Just when I started to get comfy in my cushy, padded desk chair and oversized office, the company's board and founder started to look at alternatives to being a NASDAQ-listed company.

Enter acquisition #4, public–private:
In October 2011, the Carlyle Group and Hellman & Friedman entered into a $3.9 billion deal to convert PPD private, and it was one of the largest private equity deals struck in that year. This was an incredible achievement and success for the founder, and any of the early employees and investors.

I'm clearly oversimplifying things here, but the general

goal of taking a company private is to refine and polish the already successful organization into an even leaner and more profitable venture for a future sale down the road. The next chapter digs much deeper into this.

The potential conflict here was that the Innovation group I led tended to spend a bit more than other groups, and were slightly irreverent (in a beg-for-forgiveness-later manner)—but it also leveraged many resources throughout the company. It was obviously challenging when each department was asked to do more with less, at least for the short-term.

Despite the many warning signs, I re-energized the team, made necessary changes where needed, and pressed on. That is, of course, until the concerns began to outweigh the positives.

I remember it like it was yesterday—the day my manager candidly mentioned that things were likely to get uglier and I might want to start exploring to see what else was out there. Hint, hint. . . I was fortunate to have such an open relationship with him and others on the leadership team and certainly trusted and appreciated the candor. I knew that regardless of what happened in the days and months ahead, they had my back.

So, what's next?

8

SIMULATED SUCCESS:
THE WEBMD ACQUISITION

"It's not about ideas. It's about making ideas happen."
—Scott Belsky

Why not a start-up?

From 11,000 to 11—Godspeed!

I had a friend and former colleague who worked for TheraSim, a small healthcare simulation software company located in Research Triangle Park in the Raleigh-Durham area, and decided to take a closer look.

I was attracted by the small team, relaxed and laid-back culture, and can-do, I'll-make-this-shit-happen-no-matter-what, infectious attitude that permeated through the walls. As you can imagine, this was quite different from my previous employment in a company with casual Fridays. So, I jumped aboard to help them with their mission to educate physicians around the world through simulation.

The reality is, most start-ups fail. So, this new opportunity offered tremendous risk—but also a sense of unified mission where a small group of folks were navigating through uncharted waters. The hunger of the team to succeed and overall energy definitely tipped the scales in my decision. So, I joined as a member of the management team as a creative director. Initially, I was responsible for overall product UX, design, and marketing; however, later on, I moved to software and product development roles.

Early on, I sometimes felt as though my main job was to keep the COO and founder from killing each other (with words, of course). I'm joking and being a bit flippant here, but I am not too far off. Their ideas concerning the approaches and processes that needed to be followed did not often fully align. This isn't an uncommon situation in small companies, between founders or the C-Suite. Interestingly enough, the issue worked itself out later when the founder left to focus on other endeavors.

You have to remember, small companies operate differently, and when you lose a big sale or a key client—or worse, an entire quarter of sales—the stress of sustaining payroll and keeping this motley bunch engaged is seen by all of the leadership team. No business school course can ultimately prepare you for these situations, but they are incredibly rewarding.

In addition to sprouting a few more grey hairs than

I would like to admit, I learned so much navigating through this adventure. I wouldn't have traded the experience for anything in the world. Yes, even sushi served by the legendary Jiro Ono!

Our core product was a virtual patient simulation platform, and it was delivered to healthcare professionals around the world. We worked directly with Pharma, government agencies, and renowned medical schools. And we even did a significant deployment to medical schools in Africa—all with the goal of changing clinician behavior.

Acquisition #5: One of our main channel partners was Medscape, whose parent company is WebMD. The relationship between Medscape and our company was strong, and the demand for our platform was increasing at a steady pace. After considerable negotiation and due diligence, WebMD acquired TheraSim in July 2014. We became part of a large public company with an established reputation, which was frankly a household name in the healthcare industry—at least here in the States. I've always been reminded of this fact when I go to the global conferences.

For the month or so prior to the deal being announced, our CEO, Sales VP, and I were in lock step. We had regular offsite meetings to ensure the team wasn't alarmed or altered by our conversations and the latest developments prematurely. During this due diligence process, our focus seemed to change from selling and delivering to preparing for an acquisition. In addition, I noticed we were being discouraged from pursuing deals with schools and nonprofits during this period. That's what happens in M&A, when their other priorities become your priorities; it is pretty standard operating procedure. Still, we were excited to make the acquisition work. . . and did.

Following the deal, we were fortunate and only took a few direct hits to staffing. In the transition, we lost our sales and marketing directors, and our office manager. When your team is already so small to begin with, any hit to staff can affect the group—but fortunately, each of them received generous packages. They all quickly rebounded and found other opportunities. If we would have had HR or Finance roles, they too would have met the same fate. You have to remember that all of these roles and groups already exist (in great numbers) at larger organizations. In a small acquisition, they are generally considered redundant.

Our acquisition has been one of WebMD's most successful to-date. I am extremely proud of this achievement and wear it as a badge-of-honor.

Acquisition #6: In late 2017, Internet Brands/K.K.R. acquired WebMD, taking us private in what can be best described as a merger of equals. Internet Brands has its headquarters in Los Angeles, whereas WebMD has its headquarters in NYC. My satellite division of about 40 developers, designers, medical directors, and simulation experts is based in NC's progressive Research Triangle Park.

At this point, was this acquisition really a surprise? No. Think about it. I'd gone through three major moves and multiple address changes during my childhood. I had witnessed six corporate acquisitions in a two-decade career. I moved on, adapted, and thrived.

I can tell you that any difficulty you've had in your personal life can serve you well in navigating the uncertainty and chaotic conditions in the business world—while going through an acquisition in particular. If you've experienced death, divorce, or dislocation so far in life, those experiences have taught you something valuable. As grim and tough as it was to experience them at the time, trust me when I tell you that you have been enriched.

Deep down, you should know that you have what it takes to get through this. Call it adaptive resilience, resourcefulness, or self-advocacy—the self-knowledge and coping skills you've gained are a considerable advantage. They will set you apart in how you respond to the events that follow an acquisition.

But what if your life has been incredibly stable, with one mailing address in your childhood, parents who've remained married . . . and you've only had one job since your college graduation?

Well, you don't have to worry. Remember all those experiences I recounted in these past couple of chapters? They might not be your story, but what I have learned along the way with these diversified M&A experiences will save you from having to struggle through them. In essence, you can learn what I have learned and keep the grey hairs from prematurely showing up.

NO UNICORNS HERE: THE FOUR HORSEMEN OF THE APOCALYPSE

"Anything worth doing is worth overdoing."
—David Letterman

You know the famous cartoon—the one with a big fish eating a smaller fish, but right behind the big fish there is an even bigger fish ready to devour it? That is the story of M&A. There's always another big fish out there who is hungry. The moment your predator gobbles you up, they're made equally vulnerable.

But it's not just about the big fish consuming the smaller fish in the pond.

Sometimes, in M&A, there's a twist on this big fish-little fish acquisition model. What if you have two big fish of about the same size, facing each other with their mouths wide open, clearly puzzled? This "merger of equals" is a curious thing.

Which fish becomes the top dog? Stay tuned to know the denouement to this strange mystery.

M&A deals come in a variety of sizes and flavors. It's like visiting the cereal aisle in your grocery store or considering all the craft beer options at your local brewpub. (While we are on this subject, if you are ever in Raleigh, NC, please stop by and check out my good friends at Trophy Brewing. You can thank me later!).

In 1989, Anthony Buono and James L. Bowditch in *The Human Side of Mergers and Acquisitions* cited three examples of what they called "combinations": a merger of equals between two banks, a smaller grocery business acquired by a large conglomerate, and a joint venture between two computer service start-ups.[11]

The goal of each "combination" in the book was the achievement of organizational efficiency. It was merely a management play. Back in 1989, Peter Drucker and Tom Peters were the leading business gurus—but it was an era in which the personal computer was just evolving and there was no Internet or global smartphone usage. No one used the terms "social media" or "agile software development."

Three decades later, however, technology has transformed how a business operates and performs. The reasons for M&A are more financial and strategic. Today's deals are about adding value and firepower to a company by:

---

[11] Buono, Anthony F., Bowditch, James L.: "The Human Side of Mergers & Acquisitions" (1989), BeardBooks

- Acquiring new technology or building a digital strategy
- Striking transformational deals
- Engaging in smaller and strategic acquisitions

The new 800-pound gorilla in the room is the private equity firm. The scenario comprises taking a public company private to fix its lagging revenues and boost EBITDA and the P/E ratio, thereby creating a premium valuation for the next buyer. That's the only way in which the private equity firms can return a high yield to their investors.[12]

An acquisition might not be similar to the Apocalypse, but it's in the same neighborhood. The Four Horsemen of the Apocalypse are said to represent the following:

- Conquest (white)
- War (red)
- Famine (black)
- Death (green)

Well, at least we got one right. Can you guess which one I'm referring to here?

I'm going to repeatedly reference four types of deals that I find exemplary to understanding how to survive and leverage an acquisition. Each scenario is purely fiction, even though it may have some basis in fact.

---

[12] www.wallstreetoasis.com

Scenario 1: "Goliath," "Whale, Inc.," or "Big Gulp"

In this scenario, a small entrepreneurial technology company with 30 employees is acquired by a $3B publicly-traded global technology business in the classic "build or buy" model, accelerating R&D and making the larger company more competitive with respect to its product offerings to customers.

The culture of the much larger acquirer is considered to be more formal and "corporate," yet there are still vestiges of risk-taking entrepreneurs among some of the long-term employees who remember when it, too, was a start-up in someone's garage. The other main difference is that everything is geared toward the spirit of Wall Street—that is, the steady drumbeat of quarterly earnings and the practice of keeping shareholder activists away from the boardroom.

Scenario 2: "Private Equity"

In this scenario, a mid-sized public healthcare company is taken private. The rationale is that the stock price is lagging and management has shown little capacity for figuring out new markets and product development in response to competitors' innovation. Therefore, the private equity firm intends to cut unnecessary expenses (especially headcount), raise EBITDA, and flip the company to another owner within five years, give or take. Although the pressure from Wall Street is absent in this instance, in its place there is a culture that will reward mavericks and risk-takers. It has little patience for staff members who are considered dead weight and clock watchers. Managers are expected to innovate first and ask permission later. If you need someone to tell you what to do next, you probably won't last very long.

Scenario 3: "Parity" or "Siblings"

This acquisition comprises a merger of equals between two firms that provide Point of Sale software for the fast food and "fast-casual" dining industry. Suppose Company A has a technology contract with Debbie's, which is the third-largest hamburger chain, whereas Company B has an exclusive deal with Kings, the second-largest U.S. burger chain. Together, they can go after the largest chain in the world: Golden Arches. Company A has come up with a Bluetooth table side-ordering platform for the fast-casual dining industry, whereas Company B has figured out a sophisticated AI/RFID solution for ensuring supply chain and food safety. Any division involved in unique product development and those operations will survive, especially if it will help win the Golden Arches account. However, anyone in marketing, support, finance, or HR has a 50 percent chance of having their job eliminated due to the redundancy of their designations.

Scenario 4: "Under New Management" or "New Owner"

This is a small business scenario, but one that is familiar to many. It's very similar to my experience of working for the print shop.

Padrino's Pizza is a chain of eight pizza restaurants that was started by an entrepreneurial family. One enterprising cousin (Sal) not only runs his restaurant, but also started a pizza supply/wholesale company named Sauce Solutions in the 1990s. The company sells pizza-making equipment and ingredients to the eight family-owned Padrino Pizza stores at a slight discount, plus to the 200 other restaurants in the Northeast U.S. It employs 30 people in sales, warehousing and trucking, and back-office functions.

Sal plans to sell his wholesale business to Ted, a 42-year-old telecommunications executive who was recently let go in a telecom merger. Ted used to work for Sal in college and, therefore, he understands the business. Ted has already worked under a contract as the general manager for a month, getting to know the employees, customers, suppliers, and the inventory—and the finances to make the transition smoother.

Sal has a two-year earn-out and will continue as President. The sales of Sauce Solutions' products give him financial liquidity for something that he built from scratch. Moreover, he has cash flow from the original pizza parlor he started in the 1980s. No one will lose their job in this acquisition, as it's merely going to comprise a change in ownership. Ted uses his severance as the down payment, as he is going to buy a job to replace the one he lost.

Now that we have listed the four types of acquisition scenarios, let's move on to yours!

10

THE GREAT BIG OL' BEAR HUG

"If you just work on stuff that you like and you're passionate about, you don't have to have a master plan with how things will play out."
—Mark Zuckerberg

Acquisition Impact Continuum

An acquisition will impact you in 10 different ways, as illustrated above, and some of them might occur simultaneously. Or, things may start out promising and quickly move to the center or all the way to the other end. Acquisitions are just like snowflakes and fingerprints—no two are exactly alike.

When friends or colleagues (or therapists) advise you to "embrace the opportunity," you might be clenching a stuffed panda or a hungry grizzly bear. Hug them at your own risk!

There can also be the sense of an alien invasion, especially if a larger entity acquires you in a Whale scenario in which strangers from another business world are now your bosses.

They don't dress like you, they don't talk like you, and they don't act like you. They order the most expensive entrees on the menu, fly business class, and put everything possible on the expense account. Or, alternatively, they act as if the CFO is nearby with a taser, ready to zap them on any extraneous business purchase.

They even speak a different language, especially the ones who hail from public companies. You might need a translator at your first staff meeting, as they toss around terms such as SOX, EPS, Section 302, Section 404, and "market cap" around in the manner that you used to talk about EBITDA and "annual run rate." They are terrified of the SEC and scoff at how easily you used to run things in your loosey-goosey private company.

You are now subject to new policies, practices, and politics, and, perhaps, new software for lead tracking and project management. You and your team are the lines from 106 to 114 on the fourth tab of a spreadsheet to the acquirers. Their executives who make decisions about your future have never met you or, if they have, they don't have the time to re-interview you. They are most likely to know nothing about your background, experience, work ethic, initiative, or any element of your contribution.

Your company might have been bought for its technologically-advanced products or lucrative customer list and savvy sales organization, and you might have been a major factor in creating that value or culture of innovation. Unfortunately, the acquirer can only see what's on paper or, at best, an organizational chart that is outdated by two years. The nuances and relevant details were not a part of the deal-making, and they will not be a part of the transition team's scope.

An M&A article in the *Harvard Business Review* estimates that approximately one-third of workers are considered redundant following a merger or acquisition.

Even if you keep your job, you have no idea if your bonus, vacation days, pending promotion, or office location is at risk. In such tumultuous times, it might be something as simple as mileage reimbursement that sets off a subtle reaction or outright fury.

A 2017 *Harvard Business Review* article titled "Managing Yourself: Surviving M&A" observed that "Most people tend to fixate on what they can't control:

who is let go, reassigned or relocated. In our studies, we've found that individuals faced with organizational upheaval have much more power over what happens to them than they realize."

In response to an acquisition, most managers "below golden parachute level" take a sober, head-down approach to their jobs, as they are unwilling to risk speaking up or rocking the boat. Others jump straight into updating their LinkedIn profiles and resumes and hitting the networking circuit (through lunch, coffee, and golf meetings), thinking that this comprises proactive behavior.

A third and truly proactive alternative is to embrace the change and use it as leverage for a career leapfrog or, at the very least, perform an assessment of the professional priorities and opportunity for personal growth, which is often referred to as "psychological income."

Marks, Mirvis and Ashkenas in the *Harvard Business Review* found that some of these "third rail" opportunists describe the outcomes as "exhilarating" and "the best thing that ever happened to me."[13] Based on my experience, I wouldn't go quite that far. However, what I have found is that I am much further along (and happy) in my career than I thought I'd be. I'm not sure where I'm going to land in a year, but it has the possibility to stretch me beyond where the status quo would have taken me.

[13] Marks, Mitchell Lee, Mirvis, Philip, Ashkenas, Ron, "Surviving M&A" *Harvard Business Review*, March-April 2017

You see, just 15 years ago, I was a scrappy web/systems developer at a pharmaceuticals research company. Now I run the simulation and development arm at WebMD—a "market leader in online health," to quote a press release. And, now, thanks to the recent transaction, I get to tap into the expertise of the ten or more technology companies that comprise Internet Brands and the brain power at that company's parent, KKR, a leading global investment firm. KKR & Co. Inc. manages multiple alternative asset classes, including private equity, energy, infrastructure, real estate, credit, and, through its strategic partners, hedge funds. They continue to create incredible growth and opportunities for countless companies. Speaking of tailwinds, KKR is about the strongest you can ask for.

A great place to be!

I have noticed the following three beneficial attributes of KKR right away:

- Greater openness to take risks and make mistakes
- Willingness to invest in new systems and talent
- Stronger desire and ability to grow through additional acquisitions

There are opportunities for growth in staying in a public company that is going private. You finally get Wall Street off your back. With a patient private owner, you can invest and have a down quarter or two, as long as you make up for it on the other side. You can actually be strategic and follow-through on more "Big, Hairy and Audacious Goals" (BHAGs).

When you're a part of a small company that has been acquired by a larger company, you have access to tools and talent, brand firepower, and a company checkbook. You get to leave bootstrapping behind.

The new owners have deep pockets and can raise more money, if needed. No one sweats while making payroll. Sometimes, you can fly in business class on a long trip. Moreover, you might get reimbursed more quickly for your airport parking expense. I'm not saying that you get to fly first class all of a sudden, but there is a noticeable difference when you go to work for a larger public company.

Opportunities are even present when you have a change of ownership in a small mom-and-pop operation. Heck, I got a 37-cent raise in my hourly pay and learned more than I ever wanted to about steakhouses. ;-)

The new owner might be just as cash-strapped as the previous owners, but, at least, their approach is fresh. They want to be out there every day and they value your contribution.

There is a lot to be said for a fresh set of eyes addressing an issue or observing an organization.

Many times, people involved in the problem can't see the forest for the trees. Because they are consumed by the day-to-day operations, the bigger picture is lost on them.

You have to approach something with open arms to embrace it. You have to let your guard down and get rid of every defense mechanism that might be holding you back. I may need to slow down slightly on my 2018 projects. I might have to travel a bit more to Los Angeles instead of New York. I might have to bite my tongue once or twice in meetings or check my ego in the downstairs lobby, which demonstrates my emotional intelligence and resolve to not give into my fears.

Imagine yourself walking up to a big fluffy grizzly bear and giving it a long embrace. It's not too scary, right?

11

ADAPT LIKE COACH K

"The ability to adapt is key in everything."
—Coach K

The name Michael William Krzyzewski might not mean much to you, even if you could pronounce it correctly.

Krzyzewski, who is also known as "Coach K," has been the men's basketball coach at Duke University since 1980. During almost four decades, he has led the Blue Devils to five NCAA Championships, 12 Final Fours, 12 ACC regular season titles, and 14 ACC Tournament championships. Coach K has also coached in the U.S. men's national basketball team, leading them to three consecutive gold medals in the 2008, 2012, and 2016 Summer Olympics.

Even though I work in Durham, North Carolina, and have lived in the area for many years, I have never formally met Coach K. The closest I got was at a rehabilitation center in Durham, where his relative and my grandmother were staying years ago. We crossed paths a few times in the hall or around the facility. However, I respected his privacy, and that was the extent of it. I'm not exactly sure why I felt the need to bring that up now. But, I guess, I want to highlight that whether it's on the court or the home front, the ability to weather the storm is what separates the great from the good.

Coach K has over 1,000 wins as a coach. The factor that distinguishes Coach K from other coaches in team-building is how he adjusts the play on the field according to his players' individual strengths at any given moment (on or off the court) and how each player interacts with his teammates.

He's also aware of how adaptability is tied to learning styles. He adapts his communication style based on how the players actually learn, whether that is through the auditory, visual, or kinesthetic mediums. He might use voice inflection and volume with auditory learners, ask visual learners if they can see the point he's trying to make, and hand the kinesthetic learners the ball and have them walk through the play.

Most powerfully, Coach K allows players to take on roles other than those for which they are famous. The Los Angeles Lakers' Kobe Bryant is an offensive machine. However, when he first joined the U.S. men's team in 2008, he mixed it up.

Bryant asked Coach K to let him play defense and

"guard the best player on every team" that they face. By working on his defensive skills, Bryant expanded his range and modeled adaptive behavior for everyone.

I can't help but state that this also threw off the opposing teams who had typecast Kobe Bryant as an offensive threat. Coach K's openness to this new possibility opened the door to a higher potential for the team victory. Kobe Bryant was now a double-threat and felt empowered by his ability to take on a new role.[14]

Disclaimer: I think it's important to note here that I'm by no stretch of the imagination a diehard basketball fan, even though I live in the heart of ACC country. I am well aware that this statement is considered blasphemous by many, but I had to keep it straight with you. That being said, I love watching games live and will jump at the opportunity to participate in March Madness challenges (although I may need to ping a friend for advice).

Science has supported what Coach K is teaching about adaptability on the court.

In fact, a research paper just published in the *Journal of Retailing and Consumer Services* reports on a study that looked at the factors that help create adaptability in employees, in general, and in the frontline staff, in particular. The researchers looked at over 700 workers and measured their level of adaptability, their level of

---

[14] https://www.linkedin.com/pulse/how-coach-k-wins-consistently-sanyin-siang/

job satisfaction, and their performance and emotional intelligence. They discovered that people with higher levels of emotional intelligence and emotional resilience are significantly more likely to be able to adapt to new and changing situations.

Moreover, people with higher levels of emotional intelligence are more likely to be able to empathize (showing sensitivity to the perspective and feelings of others). They are more likely to be able to regulate their own emotions (emotional resilience) in the face of change and shifting requirements of the job. This is exactly what happens during an acquisition.

There is evidence that demonstrates that people with better emotional resilience (emotion regulation skills) tend to be able to reappraise situations more quickly and alter their view and appreciation of the situation as circumstances change.

Both emotional intelligence and emotion regulation skills have also been shown to help people deal better with conflict, both interpersonal conflict and things such as conflicting demands (the old company's culture versus the new company's expectations).

People with better levels of emotional resilience (emotional intelligence) and emotion regulation skills tend to perform better as both verbal and non-verbal (body language) communicators. Non-verbal communication is huge in the "information desert" that is formed in the time that follows an acquisition, when communication is restrained or undertaken in, what is, in essence, a foreign language.

Finally, people who are more adaptable tend to have greater job satisfaction. There is a documented link between job performance and adaptability over the long-term.[15]

This study tells me that having adaptive qualities is beneficial no matter what, even if your company isn't being acquired anytime soon. Therefore, if I'm adaptable, I will have a much better chance of identifying and embracing the opportunities that the acquisition represents. Making a case for adopting flexibility in your professional life was never this easy!

---

[15] https://www.oxford-review.com/how-to-develop-adaptability-in-the-workplace-new-research/

12

UNCERTAINTY: THE CAGE MATCH

"My parents didn't want to move to Florida, but they
turned sixty and that's the law."
—Jerry Seinfeld

Dealing with the uncertainty of an acquisition can
make you feel as if you are wrestling a superior
opponent in a steel cage. Therefore, it's natural to be
anxious and rattled.

We have been raised to expect certainty. If you turn
in your homework assignment correctly and on time,
it can be assumed that you will get good grades. Get
good grades and you will be able to go to college. Go
to college, and you'll most likely land a good job. Earn
an MBA and your odds are even higher for achieving
success in your career.

Black-and-white thinking is fine until you hit the
gooey Gray Area known as an acquisition. This would
most likely provoke the following stream of questions
to pop up in your mind: Where is my footing? Where
do

I stand? My job? My bonus? My promotion? My pet projects? My insurance?

And the uncertainty extends far beyond the self.

- What happens to my group?
- What will happen to my boss?
- What happens to that cleaning crew that works as late as I do?
- Will there still be free snacks in the break room?

Stop and take a sober assessment. Place your hands in your lap, close your eyes, and take at least one deep breath, or perhaps, three or four. Once you've accomplished that, repeat the process. Maybe, you should try another approach and start keeping a journal. Write down your thoughts and fears in a private manner. However, if this isn't your style, dictate your thoughts into a smartphone app.

You will have to provide compassion and support yourself in the same way in which a parent might have to support a child who didn't make the traveling soccer team or faced rejection at school or in a social setting. You may have to give yourself a break, more often than you usually do, just for getting through the day or the weekly status meeting.

My editor introduced me to author and psychologist Rick Hanson, Ph.D. *(Buddha's Brain; Hardwiring for Happiness)*, who provides excellent guidance on mastering fear. He says our human brains are wired to expect the worst possible outcome. This "fear brain" (or "lizard" brain) was a prehistoric coping mechanism that kept us alive. However, we don't really need it in our modern era:

- The bad event isn't as bad as I'm likely to think
- It won't be as horrible as I'm making it out to be (this is the absolutism of negative thinking)
- I'm better resourced than I realize.

Okay, let's walk you through this dialogue. I will tell you how you can counsel yourself through the worst of it.

> **Me:** We just got bought by a Great White Corporation today. I'm going to lose my job.
>
> **Counselor:** You might not lose your job.
>
> **Me:** If I lose my job, I'm going to lose my house.
>
> **Counselor:** You may not lose your house if you are offered a severance package or you can land another job or start a consulting business or take on a part-time or "gig" economy job.
>
> **Me:** But, I might lose my house.
>
> **Counselor:** Sell everything you don't need anymore, put the rest in storage, and rent an apartment just like most people do. According

to The Pew Charitable Trusts, about 36% of us are renters. Moreover, think about this fact—you would have no more lawn to mow, leaves to rake, or snow to shovel! Think like a Japanese minimalist . . .

Me: But I might not qualify for an apartment if I'm out of work indefinitely.

Counselor: You might be able to move in temporarily with friends or family members until you can get back on your feet.

Me: But I might end up living in my car.

Counselor: Even if you do, it's not the end of the world. Some communities now have arrangements with churches in which you can park safely in the parking lot of churches and shower every morning at the YMCA. There are plenty of safety nets all around you, but you never have to use them.

Here's another objective fact. Some mergers have little or no effect, especially in a purely financial transaction in which the sellers' operations are almost entirely left intact.

Look, some level of change was going to be implemented anyway, whether there was a merger or no merger. Jobs and entire divisions are slashed even in the best of times. Your group just had a record quarter of deliverables and now you're looking at cutting headcount. . . Huh? This change just happens to be about ownership and management and, possibly, a new work culture. It is just business.

You might as well become Merger-Savvy, right?

In such circumstances, what will help you most is to try to have an objective approach as much as possible.

As I mentioned (earlier), I have a video production studio at work. We make videos for performing patient and physician simulations. We can't just shoot from the hip as it is done in the case of public access. The production quality has to be high.

Sometimes, everything goes right—the gear works, the lighting is right, the talent shows up, and most of our first takes are the final product. In such instances, you can feel that the momentum is with you. The wind behind your sails, if you will.

However, on other days, it seems as if everything is stacked against you. The gear doesn't cooperate. The talent shows up late or is distracted. An ambulance drives by, sirens blaring, or the office above us has an impromptu dance off. We might get a perfect take, but somebody might have forgotten to hit "record." There might be other bonehead stuff like that in play. However, we push through and make progress.

We ship when we say we're going to do so. Period.

Then again, some days are just absolute disasters. You can try to finesse the gear and the talent all you want, but the quality just won't show up in the finished result.

So, sometimes, it's okay and smart as a manager to say, "Come back tomorrow and we'll tackle it with fresh minds."

Namaste.

13

KENO'S NETFLIX COMEDY SPECIAL

*"I'd like to make you laugh for about ten minutes
though I'm gonna be on for an hour."*
—Richard Pryor

Sorry, I couldn't resist. . .

Traditionally, M&A is a humorless activity and it's my
mission in life to change that. This chapter follows the
one about dealing with uncertainty by design.

Humor just might be your best offensive weapon
for surviving an acquisition. However, I'm not sure
whether just having a *sense* of humor will be enough
to help you. Being able to laugh, chuckle, or snicker at
a ridiculous or painful merger moment might not be
enough.

Your coping mechanism of humor might not be
enough to withstand the impending bulldozer that's
about to take down your all-glass conference room,
your cheery collaborative space, your cappuccino
maker, and your ability to expense last night's social

outing of your staff. All of them? Yes, *all of them*.

You might need to step up and be the one who constantly generates the laughs, relentlessly being the humor headliner, the ringleader, and the impresario of Club Improv.

I'm not kidding. Get your material ready, as you have to be on stage soon!

One of the funniest things about M&A is the way in which the buyers act as if nothing remarkable has happened, just like those cats that pretend that the toy mouse is not on the other side of the couch and then suddenly pounce on it.

This nonchalance is the business equivalent of the no-look pass with an air of unruffled feathers and asks you calmly, "Why are you freaking out and pulling your hair out?"

Your world is being completely turned upside down, at least twice a day. The topsy-turvy scenario can be described as follows:

There's a new logo on the building and on your business card and new login procedures (and mandatory Holiday Party Behavior Training you have to attend to next week. However, to the new owners it's just the inevitable "winds of change blowing through."

"Change is a constant," they advise, thinking they're quoting Drucker or Covey or Robbins, and making it sound like they are pitching a revolutionary new smoothie maker on QVC. Who remembers the legendary Bass-o-Matic SNL skit by Dan Aykroyd?

Well, go get Toto and bring him into the storm shelter, Dorothy. Those are not mild ocean breezes from Aruba stirring the palm trees. That's one serious cyclone bearing down!

And what's the deal with synergy?

We'll talk more about this more positively in Chapter 25, but let's consider for a moment the concept of the synergy (or synergies) that is said to occur following an acquisition. Synergy is derived from an ancient Swedish term, which means "reduced headcount." When a CEO uses synergy in its plural form, it means that they paid twice as much in the deal as they should have.

Synergy is like the peanut butter with which you cover the big bitter pill so that your dog will take medicine. Synergy can be a choking hazard, especially, when its rammed down your throat.

I liked the Police album *Synchronicity* as a kid, but that doesn't mean I want to hear it playing in the conference room when the pink slips are being handed out.

Okay, now I feel a little better.

I've survived a half dozen deals so far, and there's probably another one around the corner or beyond the ridge for both you and me. Rather than wait for it to destroy us with its crashing waves, let's make an effort to champion it now instead when it begins to affects us. *What do you say to that?*

So, get ready to headline. You're on the stage next.

14

THE ACID TEST: WILL YOU SURVIVE, OR NOT?

"Your future is created by what you do today, not tomorrow."
—Robert Kiyosaki

In the 18th century, prospectors needed to know quickly whether they'd struck gold or not. They invented the acid test, where they'd pour nitric acid on a sample to assess their findings. Only gold would stand up to nitric acid, whereas the other metals would dissolve.

The term "acid test" is also used in corporate finance to measure liquidity. It comprises a quick calculation that is done to see whether a company can cover its short-term liabilities by converting its short-term assets to cash (without selling inventory) within a year or less.

I think the term is helpful for you, to help you analyze your chances. Following this, you can figure out what to do next in a situation in which a merger is being initiated. I promise—you won't be paralyzed.

Let's revisit the knowledge we learned from Dr. Rick Hanson— "You are richer in resources than you realize."[16]

To add to this, I can also tell you that you are more empowered than you realize.

The word "empowerment" has turned into a bit of cliché, so let's use the word "confidence" to describe what I mean. Confidence originally meant "the ability to mend or patch," which is appropriate here. Remember, we don't need you to be cocky here— you just need to be confident, clear-headed, and courageous.

In an acquisition, you likely have limited or no power at all (and, if we are honest, you didn't have much clout *before* the acquisition).

You are now dependent on an outsider who is reviewing your fate one-dimensionally on a spreadsheet. Your name is somewhere in one of the middle rows with no highlights or stars beside it. There is no time or opportunity for you or anyone in your group of direct reports, contractors, or dedicated freelancers to sell yourself or to give helpful background information.

The best you can do right now is to possess

16 https://www.rickhanson.net/notice-youre-alright-right-now

exceptional self-knowledge. This, in turn, can help you with achieving confidence and decision-making, even in times of great uncertainty. To help you along your way, we have developed an **Acquisition Fitness Score ™**, which looks at 10 factors. The formal assessment can be found in the Appendix.

The goal of this chapter is to introduce you to the key concepts and how they can guide you going forward, like a compass that aids in navigating dark forests and tricky waters.

Your **Acquisition Fitness Score ™** is a realistic analysis of your areas of strength and the areas in which you need to improve. These factors provide no guarantee that you will hold onto or excel at your job. However, they might help you remain confident and courageous when chaos and change are swirling around you.

Acquisition Fitness Score ™ (10 factors):

1. Are you working on any project or product or deal that is a critical mission for the company?
2. Do you have a leadership role in the project, product, or deal?
3. Are you in a profit center or a cost center?
4. Do you have domain and technical expertise (are you a subject matter expert)?
5. Do you possess functional expertise (that is, experience related to your job title)?

6. Do you exhibit emotional intelligence and interpersonal skills?

7. Do you have sponsors/advocates (who have remained from the previous management)?
8. Do you have sponsors/advocates (from the new owner management)?
9. Have you developed customer and strategic partner relationships?
10. Have you been headhunted recently? (market validation)

The Survival Fitness Assessment is in the Appendix and the following is our guidance based on your score:

- **70+ points:** Green Light—Go for it!
- **50–70 points:** Yellow Light—Proceed with caution
- **Under 50 points:** Red Light—It's probably in your best interest to contact a recruiter

Green Light: Open Field (Go for it!)

If your **Acquisition Fitness Score ™** is above 80 points, it's time to put up your spinnaker. You most likely have a tailwind in sailing terms.

Take a look at the new organizational chart if it's available from the integration team. If it isn't, find the buyer's organizational chart before the merger and assume that not much will change (except the elimination of duplicate positions). Assume that the operating structure of the acquiring company will remain intact, even if the players change.

The following are the six questions you should be asking yourself:

1. Where do you think you might land eventually?
2. Is there a business unit or division of your acquirer that you find intriguing?
3. If so, can you map to that?
4. Would you be willing to accept a transfer to another part of the country or an international assignment?
5. Is there a clear path to advancement?
6. Will the rising tide (the synergies from the merger) lift the boats that remain?

Press and Pursue: Five Proactive Things You Can Do when the Light is Green

1. **Physical health and mental release**. Actively pursue physical health and mental release even if it's just walking for half an hour a day. If the acquisition is conducted over the winter, make sure you get out in the sunlight when you can. Do something different during your out-of-work routine. Don't just go to a movie! Catch a touring Broadway play or a stand-up act at a comedy club. Go bowling or rent out a paintball course. Enrich your life whenever you can. Go with color and spices in your food.

Here's a simple way in which you can start your day. However, this won't work on Paleo diets. Add chopped dates, chopped walnuts, fresh blueberries, red raspberries, and sliced banana to your hot or cold cereal. Sprinkle the concoction with cinnamon and add a small splash of Almond milk or cream. It may seem silly, but take your time preparing the ingredients. Savor the variety of colors, textures, smells, and tastes. If you can transform a bowl of cereal, you can transform any part of your workday in equal measure. Amazing, isn't it?

2. **Follow your advancement mapping.** Network internally. Use LinkedIn, if you have to. Think of your assignment just like those crime procedurals in which the detectives solve a crime using a large bulletin board in the squad room with photographs, maps, and connecting pieces of string leading to the brilliant outcome.

3. **Identify your gaps.** Organize an advisory board of experts in the domain, technical, and functional areas in which you want to grow using Excel. Take these advisors to breakfast or lunch or take in a ball game together.

4. **Hire or engage a coach** or a counselor who will agree to help you with career and potential mental health issues.

5. **Link with other high-confidence peers.**
   Instead of pooling negative energy into speculative gossip and sniping sessions, assemble an informal band of "hunter-gatherers" whom you trust and who will provide peer support to achieve positive pursuits. Look for peers with expertise that is complementary to your skill-set and target especially anyone in product development, business development, marketing and sales, or operations. Stick close to anyone with "revenue," "customer acquisition," or "innovation" in their job titles.

Flashing Yellow Light: Proceed Cautiously

If you scored below 70 on the **Acquisition Fitness Score ™,** you are most likely in a situation in which your job might be at higher risk for elimination or possibly a lateral transfer or even a demotion.

Given below is a list of risk factors that could have some bearing on the likelihood of your job security. However, these are not areas on which you can improve much anytime soon.

- You are a new hire ("last in, first out")
- You work in a cost center or have a back-office function
- You are new in the role, following a promotion or lateral transfer
- You are new to the industry

- You have no direct reports
- Your boss has already been let go
- Your boss is too preoccupied with his survival to help you
- You are in a job that has a direct counterpart in the acquirer's business
- The acquirer cut down this department in its last merger
- You are paid too much for what you do (in HR compensation analysis)
- You have had a poor performance review recently
- You have been written up for a workplace infraction

Guidance for when the light is Yellow

If you are in legal, corporate communications, or human resources or in other back-office corporate functions that have become potentially redundant because of duplication, don't worry. Navigate carefully and develop best practices. Be known for your reliability and knowledge. Your diligence and attention to details of execution and follow-through skills might be the tie-breaker to nudge you over when the integration team looks closely at your department.

Go forth, be strong, and make us proud!

15

PILLOW TALK: The M&A Conversation for Spouses & Partners

"Marriage is really tough because you have to deal with feelings. . . and lawyers."
—Richard Pryor

This is the part of the book in which I will talk about how an acquisition will affect your spouse, partner, or immediate family members.

I'm certainly not a marriage counselor, but I am married and have a family and hope you find this helpful.

In the days that immediately follow the buy-out announcement, I'm probably going to be distracted and less attentive to issues such as home improvement, soccer practice, or dry cleaner pickups. I may seem less interested in anything outside of work, especially, if I care about my job and like what I do for a living.

(If I hate my job, I'm probably not reading this far in the

book, and I'm already celebrating at the beach).

Even if I'm not the primary breadwinner in the relationship, I'm still bringing home the proverbial bacon in some form on a consistent basis. So, naturally, I'm going to worry about my ability to continue that contribution to the household.

The questions in my mind are endless, and might include:

- What would happen if I lose my job?
- How much severance will I receive?
- How long will it take me to find another job?
- How much of our savings will we eat through while I look for another employment opportunity?
- Will we need to relocate?
- Should I update my LinkedIn profile and start looking for a job now?

I find that it helps to write down these questions, which can roam around in our minds in the form of anxiety. They might keep me up in the middle of the night.

It's also healthy to unburden myself of my doubts and fears and receive support in a trade-off. Isn't that what a spouse or partner is supposed to do?

In my experience, the main communication I'm likely

to receive from the acquirer is either radio silence or the generic "Don't call us, we'll call you." I might not have anyone at work with whom I can talk about my deepest fears. Therefore, I'm glad to have someone who will listen and help me process what might be an overwhelming amount of information and emotion in the form of my spouse or partner.

Having said that, don't "dump truck" this on your spouse or partner. Don't stew in the juices of anxiety, stockpile all your worries, and then let them loose the minute you walk through the front door. Trust me on this one. I know it is hard, but I have learned this lesson the hard way, and it isn't fair to your family.

Pick an uninterrupted time (and place) and calmly lay out the possible scenarios and responses you believe are the best remedies. Writing things down will give you a head start on this process. You will have already sorted things out in one pass, and it will be better suited for feedback from a caring partner.

This will also be a good time to measure how much support you truly do receive at home. Business, as usual, doesn't normally expose a relationship to this kind of emotion, anxiety, and uncertainty. Sometimes, the pressure of acquisition will expose weaknesses in the relationship and cracks in its foundation.

You want your relationship to endure the challenges; however, sometimes, a side benefit of all this stress is learning what your relationship is capable and not capable of supporting.

I'm sure that there's a seventh acquisition out there with my name on it. However, I'm glad that my partner/spouse is willing to ride alongside me and ready to help me tackle the next one.

16

THE NEW CULTURE: WHAT THEY SAY AND WHAT THEY REALLY MEAN

"Culture eats strategy for breakfast"
—Peter Drucker

Some people just have the ability to move between different realms easily. Some learn this at an early age while adapting to parents who give mixed messages or a situation in which each parent takes a different parenting approach—Dad rides a Harley-Davidson and encourages risk-taking, whereas Mom says, "Look both ways and be careful while crossing the street." You will probably take the best of both worlds and not run yellow lights once you have your motorcycle. If you paid too much attention to Mom's perspective, you might not ever leave the neighborhood. However, subscribing to Dad's worldview means you might not live past high school.

In the same way, if you respond positively to all the changes and flux during an acquisition, you will naturally stand out.

The majority of your peers and direct reports (and even your boss) may be frozen with all the uncertainty, as they will be quietly fuming or overtly hostile when faced with the disruption.

You might find yourself in the middle, straddling the old organization and the new one. Think half Honda Gold Wing and half Harley Sportster.

Previous Company Culture	You (Translator)	New Company Culture

Apart from your formal job title, you might find yourself performing a new role, which we'll call that of a translator. You're not really a mediator, yet you have the advantage of knowing both worlds and can speak to each faction calmly and intelligently.

This can happen as early as the acquisition announcement, play out during the integration period, or extend forward even though the two organizations are officially merged.

There might be formal integration committees, but you (and your group) have the opportunity to create alignment by paying attention to subtle cultural cues. Formal integration in the wake of an acquisition tends to be top-down, not always responsive. Occasionally, it can be tone-deaf.

In such circumstances, your impact on corporate alignment could be more pervasive and permanent than the official channels, as it will be rooted in emotional intelligence, interpersonal skills, and sensitivity.

"Culture eats strategy for breakfast."

This is a phrase coined by Peter Drucker that was made famous by Mark Fields, the President of Ford Motor Co. I've embraced this viewpoint while molding all the teams with which I've been involved and still agree with it to this day. However, as this relates to an acquisition, we can interpret it in two ways.

The entire deal can be diminished or undone by the acquired company's lack of understanding of the culture of the acquirer, as they just don't get it. For example, employees who have come up through an entrepreneurial culture of bootstrapping and acting as the long-shot underdog don't know how to behave when they have the capital to spend and have to work for the dominant market player.

For example, I originally built the TheraSim video studio from chicken wire and duct tape. We were a small company, so, in hack mode, I shopped at eBay for value and built the whole thing (with a green screen backdrop, cameras, and audio gear) for $12,000. That studio should be in the Bootstrapper Hall of Fame, and it all worked out just fine for our business.

However, in WebMD world, my hack studio was not going to cut it. They came in with a purchase order for real construction materials and professional contractors, and, probably, they spent 10 times as much as I did as a bootstrapper. Yes, 10x! Now, our studio has a sprayed-on acoustic ceiling and double-walled soundproofing made of a special composite that absolutely ensures the best possible noise reduction.

Today, the budget for building my old studio could barely buy you one camera from my new operation. The production values are phenomenal, as WebMD needed it to be, given its brand value and reputation.

To get in sync with the acquirer's culture, pay attention to social cues and the level of formality. Is your new owner more or less corporate? Previously, you may have had the latitude to pursue ideas and projects on your own initiative. However, now, you may need permission.

- Does the C-Suite wear jeans or suits?
- Do they prefer opensource to cumbersome enterprise contracts?
- What is their tolerance for experimentation and making mistakes?
- Is levity and candor welcomed or discouraged?
- Are management retreats at cloud-covered villas in Switzerland or rustic lodges in Sedona?

Alternatively, the acquirers can be equally insensitive to the culture of the company that they just bought. They could easily erode value by handcuffing a nimble entrepreneurial company with unnecessary rules, protocols, policies, and other risk-averse restraints, thereby effectively killing the goose that lays golden eggs.

The previous, smaller organization might have had a more fluid, loose style of communication. This worked because of the lack of those pesky impenetrable silos.

To put this differently, the old company might have operated like an improv group, whereas the new company expects you to follow the script word-by-word. Or, it might go the other way, and your new entrepreneurial owners might be the loosey-goosey or laissez-faire types, and if you insist on operating "by the book," it might frustrate them.

Communication works wonders

Now, there might be corporate divisions that truly form dividing lines. You might need to over-communicate and make the extra effort to ensure that all stakeholders are included.

Maybe, you have just entered the wonderful world of Wall Street and all of its lovely scrutiny and guidelines if your new owner is a public company. In this new world, everything must now be run through iron-clad gates that are manned by legal and finance guards.

However, on the other hand, if your public company has been bought by a private equity firm, your previous adherence frame of reference to "the street" may need some fine-tuning.

Is your new management hands-off or more hands-on? Look for tell-tale signs such as the number and frequency of reports and the level of detail in those reports. In a more entrepreneurial culture, there tends to be a high tolerance of risk. On the other hand, in a more corporate culture at the mercy of the Sarbanes–Oxley Act, considerably more attention is paid to risk aversion and, at the very least, risk mitigation.

Here's an example of what I was recently dealing with. When I worked for a start-up, we might recruit, hire, and bring someone onboard within two to three weeks or, in some cases, if they were unemployed, in less than a week. We had hard roles sometimes and it took much longer, but generally the process was that fast.

But the same process might take us six to 16 weeks in a corporate environment, because of the thorough justification process and workflow process. Your need to hire someone remains exactly the same, but your ability to do so could be hampered. Now, I recognize that this is yet another first-world problem, but it is your new frame of reference. Get creative, leverage your network by marketing your roles on LinkedIn, and make the best of it!

Listen to the nuances of language and social code as proxies for the new culture. "ASAP" might mean that you have a week if you need it or "take all the time you need" might actually mean that you should get the task done by the end of the day!

You will have new metrics and Key Performance Indicators (KPIs). Make sure you know what they mean and what is expected of you, as you may need to translate those for your team members.
A more formal corporate acquirer could mean that more emphasis would be put on policies, especially, those that relate to travel and expense reimbursement.

A larger or public company will probably have more regulatory requirements placed on them. So, expect to attend a lot more training sessions on compliance and HR issues. This is especially critical if you are in the financial or pharmaceutical industries.

If your company is a high-growth entrepreneurial venture that has been bought out by a large, established corporate entity, do whatever you can to tweak your entrepreneurial swagger and understand the new culture and protocols acutely. This isn't the time to be a pirate!

Remember this, unless the acquirer is about to kill your product or service and ingest your customers (this does happen fairly often), it is in the best interest of their investors to make the deal work. They have spent many, many hours on conducting research and performing due diligence, and that is before spending all the cash.

Figure out the new tools and rules and then discipline the creativity and instincts that might have been integral to your success previously. If you run your sales team loosely with verbal shorthand and low documentation, make sure that you over-communicate and report even the seemingly inconsequential details. They might hold more value than you realize.

As one of my favorite characters, Woody, said in *Toy Story*, "There's a new sheriff in town." The tail might indeed be wagging the dog and you might find yourself bristling at all the paperwork and protocol regulating your day.

However, no one really loves seeing a sheriff, especially on the side of the road with their radar gun out. I've always opted for having a more light-hearted and humanized view of the new owners as a new momma and poppa. That might be a stretch if they are a multi-billion, multi-national conglomerate based in China, but it's worked for my teams and me.

17

AIR COVER: DOES YOUR BOSS HAVE YOUR BACK?

> "No individual can win a game by himself"
> —Pelé

Former Boss

Say "goodbye" to the former boss.

There is a possibility that your previous manager is no longer in the picture. He or she may have been let go, or they might have bailed out ahead of a possible firing.

However, not every manager gets early retirement, a golden parachute, a promotion, or a plump position in the new company.

So, there's a good chance that your boss (and their boss) is still around.

A previous boss still hanging around with an uncertain

future could make you more emotionally secure than a boss who's only navigating by speculation and trying to read the tea leaves.

If you feel good about your prospects (based on your self-assessment), this could create some tension, as the traditional roles might be reversed.

Meet the New Boss

You might have a new manager sent over from the acquiring company.

Your job with a new boss would necessitate you be as open, transparent, and cooperative as possible. Pay attention to your verbal and non-verbal body language. Over-communicate and make sure to understand any requests or assigned tasks fully. Ask your new manager to repeat instructions, write them down, and assign owners, deliverables, and deadlines to each one.

Moreover, don't miss a milestone—strive to under-promise and over-deliver. Stay positive and work on building their trust. You got this!

Remember, there is no wrong answer.

If you somehow irritate or alienate your new bosses and you have to leave, maybe it wasn't a good fit in the first place. After all, you never applied to work at the acquirer's company. You accepted a job at a company that no longer exists. It's gone for good.

If you have an idea, don't keep it to yourself. This is where you might want to use the "straw man" or "simulation" strategy. Sketch out a hypothetical scenario and gauge your new manager's reaction to it by speculating the following: "If we were to try X, how would that be received?"

In this way, you can demonstrate both assertiveness and deference. You are not sitting around waiting passively to receive detailed instructions on how to proceed. Unless your new manager is completely hands-off and obtuse, he or she will recognize this as a sign of your professional savviness. *Sweet!*

How secure is your new boss?

If you have a new boss, there is a lot at stake. There are probably high expectations on him or her for a fast and successful transition and integration. You can be a very helpful ally to your new boss. You know your team, the product, and possibly some of the customers and partners.

I would recommend taking the new boss out for a cup of coffee or a stroll outside the office. Whatever works for the two of you, just make sure to vacate the office and get some fresh air, if possible. On that walk, get to know them better, learn about their family, background, and even their pets' names. Don't forget to share your situation too, so that they can get to know you more.

The initiation of this process, especially away from the office, humanizes the two of you to each other. You guys will be having each other over for BBQs before you know it!

For further reading on the subject, I recommend you pick up the book, *Radical Candor*, by Kim Scott, as she provides tangible examples of this working very well.

Make a fair assessment and understand why

If your new manager has your back, you can be more assertive and use him/her as a buffer, advocate, and sponsor, and, possibly, a job reference if you are let go.

However, if your new manager does not have your best interests in mind or if they are too consumed with their own well-being, this might impact your daily sense of satisfaction. You may also notice your access to projects and product development is limited and that you are out of the loop. A less-than-supportive new manager can also jeopardize your place in the bonus plan and promotion status or, even worse, your long-term viability within the company.

The following are some signs that you are dealing with a less-than-positive boss:

1. **Your boss is distracted**. Your boss isn't giving you their full attention consistently. They may be rattled or worried about the future, even more than you are. You may notice that normal attention to details is missing or that they are no longer exhibiting the intensity in their performance of which you once knew them to be capable. You can tell they're not listening when you tell them something, as they cannot repeat what you just said back to you. The light in them has either gone out completely or it is flickering.

2. **Your boss isn't communicating.** You might find his or her door closed more often, and every day might seem to be an endurance test just to get through it. No longer are there personal greetings and small talk. You could welcome them with a smile and even some meaningless chit-chat about sports or the weather, but it is not happening. Not this month. Pay attention also to inconsistency, shifts in policy, or setting priorities that seem to have no basis in fact or grounding in the data. They are entirely whimsical and don't follow any predictable pattern.

3. **Your boss no longer seeks input or counsel** from you or the members of your group. Before the acquisition, there might have been an air of collegiality. The business unit thrived, as the

boss sought out new ideas and opinions outside the executive suite. However, now, everything is in the shutdown mode. Your boss no longer asks for input or perhaps says dismissive things, such as "That's interesting" or "I think we have that covered" when you suggest an idea on your own initiative.

4. **Your boss is controlling information.** This "command and control" approach only serves to alienate team members. When key information is provided on a "need to know" basis, rumor and gossip become the workaround. Consequently, projects might get stalled, as there is no guidance.

5. **Your boss becomes a dictator.** This is probably the highest level of escalation, and it's probably the last resort. People don't always choose to be bullied or take a defiant "my way or the highway" stance. The boss probably feels that he or she was forced into this position by overwhelming pressure and a lack of emotional maturity to deal with the acquisition pressures in a constructive manner. When you have to start watching what you say, when there is an atmosphere of fear, or when your boss is volatile and unpredictable, it's a clear sign that things are unraveling above you. Beware! The "Lizard Brain" has taken over.

6. **Group morale is low**. When the manager is dismissive, uncommunicative, or even dictatorial, most people pick up on that and are less likely to be open themselves. The "energy suck" is contagious. Conversations and ideas go into a black hole and never emerge. In this scenario, people tend to give up, share and collaborate less, watch the clock, and resign from jobs. New ideas die and everyone, especially the company, loses. It is a sad day.

If you are experiencing any of this with your boss, now isn't the time to quit. It might be smarter to sit tight, react less, and wait out the storm. Your boss might be on his or her way to a meltdown, and there's nothing you can do to reverse it.

You might just have to wait it out if you really like your job and believe that your survival chances are strong. This is a test of your emotional intelligence and maturity to deal with these "behaviors" of your boss without being rattled. You got this!

The Dangerous, Erratic Boss

Sometimes, certain bosses can't handle all the uncertainty and chaos associated with an acquisition and they start behaving erratically. This can be unnerving for you and your team.

Don't retaliate. Stay cool and document the process.

Document everything this manager does that appears questionable, inappropriate, or which can be deemed as behavior that is not suitable for being exhibited by the leadership, workplace, or the brand.

Ask your other colleagues who have been affected by the behaviors of this boss to also document everything they see. Moreover, contact your company's human resources department and discuss the issues.

Remain professional. Avoid water cooler gossip. It will only reflect poorly on you as you vent your frustrations.

In addition, avoid informal email chit-chat with colleagues about your manager while on company time and the company's server. This includes email, company text messages, Google hangouts, and even the beloved Slack.

Keep it clean!

18

CALL OF DUTY: TAKING CARE OF YOUR GROUP

"Coming together is a beginning. Keeping together is progress. Working together is success."
—Henry Ford

Your team is fine during peacetime (the time before an acquisition). You have provided support, mentoring, and resourcing, and, after a while, they don't really need you.

An acquisition changes everything.

When your team gets in a firefight in the jungle or is pinned down on some remote mountaintop firebase that is exposed to enemy fire, it's time for you (as the boss) to get ready for battle. You might either need to go and fight it out alongside them, extract them from the landing zone, or lead them through the jungle to safety.

This is your call of duty.

An acquisition is hierarchical in nature. The boards of the two companies agree on a sales price, the timeline, and the new line-up in the C-Suite. The announcement is made at a press conference, the regulators and the bankers approve the deal, and the lawyers draw up the papers. After the ink dries, all the top dogs all go out to dinner to celebrate.

Now, the fun begins. The executives who remain must execute the merger, and most of this is top-down behavior, which is driven by the senior executives or managers in human resources. It is all happening above you, just like the weather. And then, one day, it rains down and rains for weeks, with announcement after announcement, plan after plan, reassignments and job cuts, relocations, and office shifts. It's all happening at a level above you, and you can do nothing about it.

The impact of an acquisition on middle management is crystal clear on some days and vague on other days.

So, how can you help your direct reports, or, in some cases, manage your independent contractors, who are making their way through this trickle-down environment?

Whether you realize it or not, an acquisition means that you now have another new role, namely, that of an advocate and a champion of your group.

Remember that the buyer is likely to have a spreadsheet mentality. Your acquirer doesn't know your group in the way that you do. The acquirer's perspective of your company or group is limited to a line-by-line quantitative, formulaic view, which comprises mostly names and numbers. It is more than likely that there is no qualitative approach or interest in narrative depth or nuance.

Generally speaking, acquirers like to use terms such as "seamless" and "frictionless." Implementing the "playbook" spreadsheet approach to integration makes them think that they are saving time and money. It may not be true in the short term, but that is the way in which acquirers have been trained. Many of them don't know another way, and frankly it has worked for them in the past, so you really can't blame them. Their data is sound.

Respond to that spreadsheet mentality with a spreadsheet of your own. List each member of your group by name and job title and note any of the following attributes that you identify with them:

- Project experience
- Product experience
- Project and product management experience
- Subject matter/domain expertise
- Functional expertise (specific job skills)
- Professional designations and credentials
- Blogger or industry influencer

- Customer, strategic partner, or vendor relationships

I recommend that you and your team put together a compelling slide deck or, even better, a short video that could be easily distributed and consumed by all. Have fun with it!

Your new job involves identifying, packaging, and positioning the members of your team who can make a contribution. You are now in sales and marketing, and the product is your team.

You are also a therapist. Your main job is to listen and provide support. However, you cannot necessarily solve their problems, as it might be beyond your control.

Remember, the members of the group might not share your perspective or optimism. The following emotions and personal agendas may tend to dominate:

- Apprehension and nervousness
- Paralysis
- Self-centered behaviors
- Anger
- Regret and despair
- Survivor's guilt

These are some of the pretty sophisticated personal

issues with which you will have to deal, and these are definitely "above your pay grade." You might have up to 10 or 15 direct reports, which would be a heavy caseload for a trained therapist. Yet, most of it comes down to the following two very simple tactics as follows: *listening and acknowledging.* If you are a spouse or a parent, apply your successful interpersonal skills from outside the office to your work inside the office. Your "work family" will be stronger for it.

Aside from listening, acknowledging, and communicating "early and often," there are other more defined areas in which you can advocate on behalf of your group. Some of these are potentially volatile items that you need to bring up with the new management. Choose carefully amongst the following:

- Overdue performance reviews and salary hikes
- Promotions that were promised by the previous management
- Bonus or stock options that were promised by the previous management
- Vacation/paid time-off that was previously promised

Some of these might have been verbal promises, and some might have even comprised written documentation. The new management is under no obligation to honor them, but it will be wise of them to not ignore them across the board.

These are not entitlements, but rather normal business expectations, and you should address them with a strong supporting business rationale. If the new management ignores them, the company risks losing key personnel who will be very expensive to recruit, hire, and train later on.

There will also be status issues, such as those related to office location and parking spaces, which are probably best left alone.

Most of my advice in this chapter apply to a small company that is acquired by a large company, a merger of equals, or a public company that has been taken private. In all three of the scenarios above, the spreadsheet mentality prevails.

If you are in a small company with a new owner or in a company that has been acquired by another small company, your charge will be much easier. There will be less spreadsheet mentality and more opportunity for personal interaction. If the new owner doesn't make a personal visit within two months, invite them to drop by for an informal showcase of your group.

In a larger company scenario, it's unlikely that the senior management will visit, but you can extend an invitation to your new boss or someone who is at least one or two levels senior to your designation. That is both acceptable and desirable. They most likely have the best intentions but get stuck with implementing priorities and putting out big fires and the visit falls off the list. But if they blow you off your invitation completely, that may be foreshadowing of what is to come.

When you advocate professionally and assertively on behalf of your group, it provides a level of certainty and stability that didn't exist before. Your team will be more productive. They can go back to doing their jobs instead of being paralyzed by speculation and water cooler banter.

Keep your team busy.

Invent opportunities for collaboration. Take things off-site with an activity to a bowling alley, a local park, or an arcade/Go-kart place. Trust me—once you get the entire team behind the steering wheels of smelly go-karts, it is incredible how many smiles are created. The change of venue, especially, in the sunshine, will make a big difference and loosen things and the team members up.

I've heard of one very creative response in which a team held a going away party for the old logo!

So, order a cake and a gaudy metallic banner. Get everyone to sign the going away card. Pass the hat and donate the proceeds to a charity. Cry a bit on your way home, if only for a second or two. It's okay. No matter how hard you try, your therapeutic advocacy and programming efforts can't solve a poorly executed acquisition in which the new management is either tone-deaf, indifferent, or outright hostile to a humane approach.

Candidly speaking, you may have some less effective or redundant positions in your group. Someone in your group might have to leave. You might not be able to take care of every individual, so set the following reasonable goal:

I will be happy if 80% of my group excels in the new company, and it's possible that they might no longer be working directly for me.

Keep your chin up!

So . . . I felt Jerry could add some needed levity here for us.

"According to most studies, people's number one fear is public speaking. Number two is death. Death is number two. Does that sound right? This means to the average person, if you go to a funeral, you're better off in the casket than doing the eulogy."
—Jerry Seinfeld

19

KNOW YOUR LINES: ALIGNMENT WITH THE ACQUIRER

"Oh the things you can find, if you don't stay behind!"
—Dr. Seuss

In my next life, I want to be a stand-up comedian. It might also be possible in this life once this book becomes a bestseller, that is, if people select it consistently over *Harvard Business Review* at the airport bookstore! You can always recommend this book to some of your needful friends, you know? ;-)

Self-promotion aside, let's delve into the contents of this chapter without further ado.

How does a stand-up comedian carry a 20-minute set at a club or give a perfect delivery during every minute of a one-hour comedy special?

Surprise! Surprise! It has to do with knowing your lines. Did you ever notice how a comedian pauses to take the microphone off the stand, walks to either side of the stage, or takes a drink of water? This usually comes after a big laugh and is most likely a transition point.

It means that the comedian is lining up another bit or another gag from the very beginning.

The entire set for a stand-up comedian (10 to 20 pages of material) comes entirely out of his or her head. If you notice, you'll find that seasoned comedians rarely miss a word or draw a blank in front of an audience. That's because they work exhaustively on their lines so that they are fully aligned with their material.

Aligning means to arrange things in line with a specific intent and an eye for how things relate to each other in advance.

A baseball coach announces his "line-up" before the baseball game, matching his team's strengths to the opposing team's weaknesses, when possible. If the opposing team has statistically faced trouble in getting hits against left-handed pitchers, then it's an advantage to start a left-handed pitcher and shut down the other team early.

When you get new tires for your car, you have them aligned. This allows a smoother ride (comfort) and makes your tires last longer (allowing you to save money). Similarly, when you have back pain, you might seek out a chiropractor or a medical professional for an alignment that allows you to walk easily without contortion or pain.

By now, you should have a very good idea of the new

corporate culture (values, beliefs, and behaviors).

Pay special attention to the behaviors that might seem antiquated or less than productive to your acquirer. Think of how jarring it is to see someone still using a flip phone or a Blackberry these days. I'm not suggesting that you learn how to code software. But you should try to do whatever you can to demonstrate that you operate in the modern era.

There is quite a bit that you will need to interpret and figure out from the nuances. For example, when someone from the acquirer directs you to "come in under budget" on a project, does that mean barely under budget (less than 5%) or does it mean ensuring healthy savings between 15 and 30%?

You might have operated with an informal, light touch with your co-workers previously, as you knew them well and you had experienced getting things done according to your company's satisfaction. However, now you have to deal with unknown elements, which are potentially more formal. Aligning with the acquirer might necessitate approaching projects and products with more intensity and a greater sense of urgency. You may need to be more "buttoned down" in your approach. Conversely, if a private company has acquired you, you may need to become more loose and relaxed. So, is it more design agency or governmental in nature?

You may also notice some obvious redundancy in

certain roles. Do what you can to create differentiation. For example, devote yourself toward acquiring more technical depth or subject matter knowledge. Depending on the situation, you might need to be more of a specialist or more of a generalist.

People think that being a generalist means you lack focus. On the contrary, it entails keeping a wide perspective and constantly keeping your right and left flank covered, which takes a tremendous amount of focus. In addition, you have to constantly fight the urge to be hyper-specialized.

Let's say that you work in a small bank's marketing department, and you are acquired by another bank of greater size. Your prior bank excelled at having a high personal touch that engendered customer loyalty. But the large bank excels at technology and the convenience of being established in thousands of locations (ATMs and branches).

Alignment means that you invest time in learning about the other bank's strengths (technology and operational scale) while simultaneously retaining your bank's culture of facilitating a rich, personalized customer experience. Your marketing counterpart at the acquiring bank might share the same job title and responsibilities, but you would have the opportunity to influence on a far broader scale.

Learn as much as you can from your counterpart.

Become an expert at technology and in the operational scale, which means seeking out podcasts, online courses (coursera,lynda, udemy and others), YouTube videos, or mentors who can help you learn quickly. Alignment also means sticking to your guns and contributing your expertise. The acquirer bought your bank for its high-touch customer care. Make sure you share your knowledge with the acquiring teams who are stronger on the technology side of the business.

Alignment is where much of the synergies of an acquisition take place.

In a previous acquisition, we used Box cloud storage, and our acquirer did not. They were lagging behind us in adopting some cloud services. The dated Microsoft solution did exist, but it wasn't terribly user-friendly and was limited to certain pockets within the organization.

We served as a guinea pig, advising them on how to use the cloud storage, which really added a tailwind to our integration efforts. This simple, yet bridge-building encounter exposed my team to other groups in the broader organization and trust foundations started to be developed all around.

However, there will be times when true alignment isn't possible. You might have to "straddle" both cultures temporarily in such instances. Alignment will happen eventually, but you might need to operate in an environment of ambiguity for a few weeks (or months). Godspeed!

Back to our banking example. The acquiring bank may think that technology is the only answer to a business problem based on the following saying: "When you are a hammer, everything looks like a nail." Thus, there may not be room for your personalized approach to meetings.

Quite a pickle, huh? Ok, in this case, I recommend that you proceed using your acquirer's technology-solves-all approach and keep your analog wisdom at a distance. One day, it will become valued, either post-alignment or in another bank that appreciates it.

20

I KEPT MY HEAD DOWN, BUT THEN THEY FORGOT ABOUT ME

"Your future is created by what you do today, not tomorrow."
—Robert Kiyosaki

Things can be deceiving. The acquisition is over. You are sitting at your desk in your same office, surrounded by most of the same people. You have the same parking spot, your old email address, and your old business card. You may think that little has changed.

However, the reality is that you now work for a new company—one you did not choose to work for. Never forget that. However, don't give into the easy clutches of depression either.

You're not only surrounded by most of the same people, but you're also surrounded by uncertainty. It may be hard to gauge when you need to keep your head down and when to assert yourself. You don't want to be like that penguin who stays at the edge of the group—the one that is most likely to be nudged off the ice into the water where the predators can get you. However, you don't want to be the shiny new koi in the pond that is frequented by cranes either. As an aside, this exact thing regarding the koi recently happened to us at our house, so be warned and get a net to cover your pond.

Staying busy helps. The more time you have to be idle, the more time you have to worry about your future and imagine unfavorable scenarios that may not be likely to occur; however, nevertheless, it can be demoralizing.

Start small. Participate in meetings and email threads in which you feel included. Be a part of the conversation. Don't be scared into opting for silence. Add perspective and value in whichever discussion you can. Be as self-aware, positive, and helpful as possible no matter what.

Slowly expand your contribution and your range.

As a part of my product responsibility, my team and I create innovative virtual patient simulations for doctors that feature actors who play the part of the patients. I have a video production facility at my disposal. Before the acquisition, I used to send our CEO and senior management an informative and fun "highlight reel" of our quarterly accomplishments. It was highly inventive and creative, and the video might remind you of Weekend Update on Saturday Night Live. My extroverted staff who participated in it (on and off-set) loved the creative outlet. They looked forward to it and always went above and beyond. In addition, my audience appreciated how we communicated our contributions in a snackable and delightful manner. It's one of the things that made our previous company such a great place to work at.

Therefore, we retained this tradition even after the acquisition. We produced a video for the quarter that included the integration of the two companies. There were many good things that needed to be shared and we did it in the same light-hearted and professional way.

I circulated it to our entire sales and marketing organization and senior management. As always, they appreciated the humor, high production value and overall dedication to making it happen consistently (quarter-to-quarter) despite how busy the team was.

Keep 'em coming!

21

DAYLIGHT HEIST: INTELLIGENCE, INTEGRATION, INNOVATION - THREE WAYS TO CRUSH IT

"Learning and innovation go hand in hand. The arrogance of success is to think that what you did yesterday will be sufficient for tomorrow."
—William Pollard

The comedian Dane Cook has a funny bit about male behavior, which he has named "Heist." It goes as follows:

> *"Given the choice, any guy would rather be part of a heist! You know when you watch the movie 'Heat,' you're like 'I wanna do that!' You just wanna be running down Main Street with an AK-4:*
>
> *Pffff-pffff-pffff*
>
> *WHERE'S THE VAN?*
>
> *Pffff-pffff*
>
> *THE VAN WAS SUPPOSED TO BE HERE! Pffffff."*

You may not realize it, but this acquisition could be the very best thing that has ever happened to you in your career.

An acquisition is a major disruptor. It shakes things up. It opens doors that may have been closed to you previously. It could be the tide that lifts your boat.

An acquisition could be like a daylight heist for you. All you have to do is walk in, grab the loot, and walk out, and then find your getaway van.

If you scored over 80 on the **Acquisition Fitness Assessment** ™, the following are the three pragmatic areas that you can most likely influence:

- Intelligence
- Integration
- Innovation

These three impact areas are interrelated and build upon each other. Gathering intelligence and organizing the data allows you to be a knowledgeable resource. Moreover, this knowledge and status naturally give you a leadership role in integration. Once the integration is in place, your intelligence also helps you identify and cultivate internal processes and external products that are ripe for innovation.

And remember, the term "innovation" is not just about technology. Financially, it means that there will be no more commodity position in the market, higher profit margins, and, possibly, a higher stock price and happier shareholders.

Intelligence Impact

So, let's start with intelligence and the distinction between primary and secondary market knowledge.

You'll want to make sure you YIU are gathering primary, real-time anecdotes and data from front-line business units, customers, and strategic partners. Pick up the phone, take someone to coffee or lunch, or schedule a disrupt day, and then take them out for drinks.

Most people rely on secondary market intelligence, which can be found in static sources such as reports, and it is stale from the moment that it is collected. The market for chemicals or raw materials can shift overnight because of some political, regulatory, or commercial activity that happened yesterday, and it is most likely that your customers' outlook would have changed with it. Meanwhile, the secondary market report that was compiled months ago by well-meaning and professional analysts lags behind by 100 or more news cycles. The focus group or task force results, even though they were considered primary research at the time, are now gathering dust.

Keep your most reliable sources close and your

responsive sources even closer.

Become proficient in understanding the details and nuances of internal workflows and customer touchpoints. For example, think about what all the possible communication channels for a merged department and which ones are best for sharing certain kinds of merger information.

The following are the ten possible channels, each with its advantages and drawbacks:

1. Email blast
2. Written materials
3. SMS texts
4. Webinars
5. Podcasts
6. Videos
7. Private social media page
8. All-hands meeting in a conference room
9. Off-site retreat
10. Off-site social events

These operational steps are critical for both operations and profitability of a business. Become a statistical genius. Every anecdote you share should have a "by the numbers" story behind it. Backup your story with what the quants call "meaningful sample size."

Be careful with surveys. In my experience, successful surveys require a subject matter expert and a considerable amount of focus and iteration to get it right. There is certainly a science behind the structure of questions, the types of answer scales, and even the flow and UX is critical. Too much open text fields make the aggregation and trend analysis close to impossible. Moreover, even if you get all of that just right, the folks whose opinion you want to know most are frequently in that group of non-responders or the middle.

Now, you're ready to translate your intelligence skill into facilitation of integration.

Integration Impact

"Execution requires a comprehensive understanding of a business, its people, and its environment."
—Ram Charan

Do you know how to execute a plan?

Many are able to draft a nice, pretty plan in a PowerPoint presentation, but few are able to get that plan to the finish line. Maybe project management is not your strong suit. Maybe you are more of a "wing it" and "shoot from the hip" kind of manager. It's possible that you thrive outside of the traditional process in which business is conducted in a structured environment.

My guidance to you is to ensure that you timeline and

task everything you can, even if it's in a simple Excel tracker without daily prompts and automated email reminders. If you own any piece of integration, you will be working within your timeline daily. Software such as Asana or Smartsheets will certainly help you here. There is no shortage of productivity applications out there, so just pick one and go!

Own the meeting invites and the follow-up for anyone who doesn't respond to the critical missions. If your contributor cannot attend, ask them to phone in or send an alternate who is prepared and has the ability to share information. As a last resort, ask your contributor to submit their ideas or plans ahead of a meeting if they cannot attend it and ask them whether you can assign a task to others in their absence.

If you run into a roadblock, barrier, or delay in your integration, figure out a constructive workaround clearly and non-emotionally instead of blaming the barriers for impeding your progress. Blaming helps no one. Identify any resources that can help you move forward. Escalate the request for help.

Remember, you're not running a popularity contest— you're trying to create a new job for yourself in the post-integration atmosphere.

However, neither should you be a tyrant or what is often popularly referred to as "the bull in the China shop." Be respectful, open, and honest and listen and withhold judgment on others who might be defensive, slow to respond, or outright obstructive.

In obstacle courses used at corporate retreats, you have to help boost people over the wall in the expectation that they will help you at the next barricade you face if you need their help. Identify and recognize those willing participants.

Make a list of your "Over the Wall" allies and your potentially obstructive team members. Some may fall into an unknown status in the middle. Your job is to pull the middle group into the "Over the Wall" group and relegate the obstructionists into the middle ground or cut them loose.

Your goal is not to win the race as a soloist. Instead you need have a winning team assembled at the finish line.

Integrations usually take three to six months and true authentic assimilation can take a year or two, which can, sometimes, be extended longer. It might be the day you stop referring to the acquisition using terms such as "us" versus "them." Ideally, that should happen with your first new paycheck, but that doesn't occur very often.

You may be asked to participate in a meaningful way or as a "show horse" to demonstrate the new synergy.

Regardless of the reason, use the opportunity

to leverage the visibility. Build and brand the communication channels to your counterparts from your acquirer, if you have the ability to suss out that kind of intimate knowledge. At the very least, use LinkedIn to map out the new territory.

The following are the six integration strategies:

1. Over-inform and over-communicate using the protocols and technical jargon of your acquirer.

2. Deal with "small-picture" thinkers and obstructionists quickly. If someone provides extra friction, trust me, it is likely to happen again. Make sure to deal quickly with the problems and gaps in trust and respect.

3. Clarify unresolved ambiguity from the original negotiations as quickly as you can. You need to know where you stand. If an assumption is made with which you don't agree, challenge it politely and professionally, and backup your scrutiny with data. This goes back to your confidence score and the level of primary intelligence that you have gathered in the self-assessment.

4. Acknowledge anxiety from your team, but reduce water cooler speculation and gossip. Don't huddle with your team separately before or after an integration meeting, as it might give off the wrong impression.

5. Take advantage of social opportunities, such as retreats and kick-off meetings. Introduce yourself to as many people as you can and send follow-up notes around areas of common interest, such as sports teams, vacation destinations, hobbies, and people you might know in common.

6. Become an anthropologist and social scientist. Study the myths, rituals, and symbols of the acquirer's business. These are powerful verbal and non-verbal cues for dealing with the new tribe. You might have worn flip-flops or colored shoelaces and colored socks in your creative, entrepreneurial start-up. However, your acquirer's attire might be marked by the professional shades of grey, black, and white.

One challenge might comprise dealing with a lack of information from the acquirer, especially, when you're in a Whale Scenario in which you had a smaller company where communication was free-flowing and instantaneous. Doors were never shut or locked and laughter was abundant. The ping pong table was out in view by all.

However, if your acquirer is larger, they might tend to be more conservative and averse to sharing information (no more public API) and might have policies and binders of Standard Operating Procedures (SOPs) documenting every little thing that is undertaken by the organization. It could feel more like a government agency if this is your first exposure to such an environment. You may hear phrases such as "that's confidential," "that's on a need to know basis," and "we will share the details when the time is right." If the information is essential to your integration project or deliverables, you can certainly request the information by being non-emotional, specific, and setting up a reasonable timeline for disclosure.

Innovation Impact

"The change brought on by M&A often opens the door to all kinds of innovation. Teams and individuals who might ordinarily have no chance to present ideas to senior leadership suddenly find themselves with access to a receptive audience, and those willing to speak up get noticed."
—Mitchell Lee Marks et. al., *HBR*, "Surviving M&A."

Your approach to innovation post-merger might be similar, but it should be reframed to reflect the new owner's business culture.

Therefore, innovation under the new management should focus on the following:

1. Quick wins (this will establish credibility)
2. Short-term revenue (within six months)
3. Bootstrapping and using little capital investment until you better understand the broader spend tolerance levels

4. Lightly resourced initiatives (in terms of staff and contractors)
5. Ship and repeat! (in the words of Seth Godin)

While the "dust is in the air," you will have a narrow window of openness and opportunity before everything settles back into, what I call, the "standard corporate cadence."

While things are still in flux, seize the chance to make a bold move or two. Despite where you are placed in the organizational hierarchy, this is your moment. **Seize it!**

Have you heard the phrase, **"Beg for forgiveness instead of asking for permission"**? This has always been my preferred approach. In one of the assignments that I had undertaken at a previous organization, our group built prototypes without gating and only sought executive approval once we had something developed pretty far along. However, once the ink was dry and the new management came along, most things had to be blessed at inception. Let's call this "Permission-Based" innovation and it just doesn't work.

After the merger dust settles, you will potentially become more concerned with approvals, budgets, and stage gates. However, what I've often found is that **more constraints and roadblocks can potentially yield even greater levels of creativity.** The constraints force your team to develop creative workarounds and come up with truly novel solutions.

When you have semi-bottomless budgets (I'm thinking big tech, pharma, and oil R&D), they can try many things simultaneously, but often those initiatives are a complete bust or turn into only offering an incremental change for the business or product.

Now, if you throw enough at the wall, you will find something that sticks eventually, but it will most likely not be a moonshot. Think about it: When your company is flush with cash, R&D efforts can be sprouted across your teams and global office locations with ease. The teams are often less vested, less hungry, and less competitive.

It is unfortunate, but it happens. The employees take on behaviors just like a spoiled teenager with a trust fund. Therefore, remember, the resistance and constraints (budget or otherwise) that you now face can lead to some amazing breakthroughs.

Get in there and make it happen!

22

GANG-RELATED: TIPS FOR TALENT MANAGEMENT

> "If you hire people just because they can do a job,
> they'll work for your money. But if you hire people
> who believe what you believe, they'll work for you
> with blood and sweat and tears."
> —Simon Sinek

This book is primarily about helping you build your "survival fitness" in the wake of an acquisition, yet your ability to pull your team (the gang) along with you for the heist will be integral to that survival. So, prepare to channel the spirit of Robin Williams' character from *Dead Poet's Society.*

In this chapter, I will touch on the topics of retention, recruitment, and dismissals and also cover in simple, non-legal terms, how non-compete agreements can work.

Retention

To lead the way, you may have to become proficient at assessing your direct reports using the fitness scale provided previously and in the Appendix.

You may have to spend time after your office hours just listening empathetically to others or coaching someone on navigating a complex assignment in which there might be ambiguous signals at play. For example, if you have been a public company and the buyer is taking you private, how much latitude does your direct report provide with respect to developing a new product, now that meeting a quarterly earnings call is no longer an issue? Your direct report may not understand all the nuances of product development under the new regime. Therefore, it may be up to you to interpret and translate new guidelines.

Moreover, what about a valuable contributor who is unnerved or unhappy and wants to quit? How can you salvage that person? This is what we might call the "talking someone down from the ledge" scenario. The "flight" response is pretty normal. They're either talking about quitting or they may have already given you a resignation letter.

There could be a lot at stake in losing someone who has a key customer or partner relationship or who is integral to a mission critical project or product. You are most likely under a hiring freeze and won't be able to hire a replacement anytime soon, let alone train someone and bring them up to speed. Recruiting and onboarding a new employee is a very time-consuming and costly exercise, but the costs of a bad hire are even worse.

The cost of recruiting, hiring, and onboarding a new employee can be as much as $240,000, according to Jörgen Sundberg, CEO of Link Humans, an employer branding agency in London. Those costs for a bad hire include recruitment advertising fees and staff time, relocation and training fees for replacement hires, disruption to projects, lost customers, damage to the brand, litigation fees, and outplacement services. Whoa!

Here's the irony of an acquisition. Your technical and domain experts end up keeping their jobs, as they might exactly be the reason behind why the company was bought in the first place. Because these experts' positions are safe, they don't have any news for a while. They watch as the redundant, back-office positions are cut down and the top dogs take golden parachutes. They wonder if they are next and tend to be the ones who update their resumes and LinkedIn profiles first and are more likely to be recruited by headhunters. These are the people who don't have to worry, yet they do.

You will need to know what "sweeteners" you have at your disposal to retain the key people. You will have to not only be able to sell the story, but also to know whether you have any financial incentives (raise, bonus, and stock options) or "psychological income" (title, promotion, workspace, flex hours, and formal recognition) in your arsenal of retention tools.

Another role in this situation is that of advocate, which entails selling your valuable direct reports to the new management and explaining the detrimental impact of this person's resignation. If you are still in the "spreadsheet" phase of the acquisition, this will be a tough sell, as the resignation will actually help in lightening the overhead load. That's one less termination that the integration team needs to worry about.

Advocating on behalf of a key team member is easier in the aftermath of acquisition when the resignation means a net loss to the headcount after all cuts have already been made. As discussed earlier, it depends on the type of merger, but, in my experience and research, this tends to comprise 8-12% of the workforce. The reality is that most, if not all organizations can afford to lose 10% of their workforce without providing any major business justification. I'm sure that there are four guys right now who are working on their Ph.D. and who have all the data to back up the rationale. If you are that Ph.D. student, let's connect!

In addition, don't be a cheerleader or advocate for staff who don't deserve it. Your advocacy reflects on your judgment. You don't want to go to bat for someone who you know or sense will make you look bad in the long run. It sounds a bit cut-throat, but you have to consider your capital when you take on retention. Talent Management is not really about management, per se. Your job is to *inspire, empower, train and retrain*. Seven out of 10 workers report that training and development is what keeps them from leaving.[17]

All the great leaders in the world's companies think and act the same way. Simon Sinek calls this phenomenon "The Golden Circle."

Recruiting

Let's say you made a job offer to someone on the day of the announcement. It might include a position that is difficult to fill because of the required experience or skills. If you have a high survival fitness score and confidence in the contribution of your group, I would say push that through quickly and onboard the talent. That may be risky for them as new hires, but, at least, you will be properly resourced for the months ahead.

This is because you probably won't be hiring much during the combination/integration phase.

Dismissals

Sometimes, you will be asked to wield the hatchet. It might not seem fair, but they are your direct reports

---

[17] https://www.thelearningwave.com/survey-shows-employees-want-more-workplace-training/

after all. Consider your ability to handle this both professionally and compassionately to be a sign of your long-term value as a manager.

Remember, these terminations will affect the morale of the direct reports that remain and will be closely watched by to your new bosses who want to see how you handle the situation. Don't underestimate the "optics" of an exit interview. Everyone knows that it's happening, and they are watching you.

Be clear about the reason, which will usually be about eliminating a redundant position. Now, most of these reductions in force (RIF) exercises come with generous severance packages that tend to soften the blow. However, each affected individual has a different frame of reference and situation.

So, proceed as humanly supportive as possible and be compassionate, sympathizing with them as if you were the one receiving the news. Preserve this person's dignity to the greatest degree that you can. There are even some rituals associated with a termination (for example, cleaning out one's desk, turning in badges and keys, and being escorted by the security guard to the lobby) that are essential to the finality of the event. Don't try to short-cut them.

If the person you are firing becomes upset, acknowledge their emotions, but don't try (trust me here) to dismiss the event's significance. The thing that most people fear has happened. Don't try to get in the way of their perceiving the harsh reality of the moment. Don't offer consolation or consolation prizes through promises, such as "I'll help you find a new job." You can certainly do that behind the scenes, and I have done just that many times, but it's not what you want to say in an exit interview. Please consult with your HR department if you have other questions or concerns.

Non-Compete Agreements

According to the U.S. Treasury Department, "Research suggests that 18 percent, or 30 million, American workers are currently covered by noncompete agreements. Even more workers, roughly 37 percent, report having worked under a non-compete agreement at some point during their career."[18] If a worker has an advanced degree, there is a 30 percent chance that they'll have to sign one.

You may be asked to sign a non-compete agreement pre-acquisition. In consideration for well-defined temporal or geographic restrictions, you should expect some form of consideration or compensation. Keeping your job is included in that consideration.

When buying a business, obtaining an effective non-competition agreement from the seller is typically a critical component of the deal to protect the buyer's

---

[18] https://www.treasury.gov/resource-center/economic-policy/Documents/UST%20Non-competes%20Report.pdf

post-closure business interests. From my research, courts review overly restrictive non-competition agreements with very close scrutiny.

Non-competition agreements that are entered into in an employment context generally need to be limited to a period of six months to three years, in connection with the sale of a business.

A non-compete clause is supposed to help protect trade secrets, which means profitability and sustainable competitive advantage. Strangely, less than half of the workers with a non-compete agreement report having access to any trade secrets. If there's lack of access to trade secrets, the signing the non-compete isn't really necessary.[19]

In North Carolina, a non-competition agreement was entered into in connection with the sale of a business must (1) be in writing, (2) be reasonable as to time and territory, (3) be reasonably necessary to protect the legitimate business interests of the purchaser, and (4) not interfere with the interests of the public.

Reasonable as to Time & Territory

State courts consider the geographic scope of and the length of time for which the restrictions last when determining whether a non-competition agreement is reasonable.

---

[19] https://obamawhitehouse.archives.gov/sites/default/files/non-competes_report_final2.pdf

For example, a restriction on competition that lasts for three years may be reasonable within one geographic territory (for example, North Carolina), but it might be unreasonable within a larger geographic area (for instance, the South eastern United States).

Geography may mean a specific location and the area surrounding it or it may loosely refer to all the locations where the business exists, for instance, where the majority of the customers are located. The restrictions cannot include areas where the seller does not have customers or does not conduct business.

Protection of Legitimate Business Interests

The restriction should only cover the business in which the seller was engaged and, therefore, for which the seller has a competitive advantage.

Greater restrictions may be appropriate for executives or other high-level employees of the acquired business to protect sensitive information about the business or its customers or industry information that would be known to senior employees. It is also difficult to support a non-competition agreement that seeks to restrict a person from competing in an area in which he or she did not perform services or have expertise.

The Interest of the Public

If a court finds that the elimination of the seller's

competition would be detrimental to the public interest, it will be less likely to enforce the agreement.

Other Considerations

If the buyer is seeking to enter into non-competition agreements with any individuals who are not receiving sales proceeds (e.g., employees), then it will be particularly important to provide some consideration to the plight of such individuals.

If the deal is structured as an asset sale, then employment with the buyer is treated as new employment and, therefore, a non-competition agreement would be supported by consideration in the form of such new employment. However, in a transaction that is structured in the form of a merger or stock sale, an employee is treated as being continuously employed throughout the closing of the transaction and, as a result, the buyer would need to provide additional consideration to the employee in exchange for signing a non-competition agreement.

Like I've said before, I am not an attorney or expert on non-competes, so for more information or clarification, please consult a professional.

23

THE REAL BOSS: MANAGING CUSTOMER AND STRATEGIC PARTNER EXPECTATIONS

"To build a long-term, successful enterprise, when you don't close a sale, open a relationship."
—Patricia Fripp

I have always told my team the following: "At the end of the day, without sales, we won't have a team for much longer." Regardless of where you are placed in the organizational hierarchy and in which department, your contribution has an indirect impact on sales and the overall experiences of the clients.

One of the safest places you can occupy during and after an acquisition is in a customer-facing role. "Customer" is code for "revenue" and "profit," whereas "future revenue" is tied to share price and shareholder value in a public company.

Working with customers in a smaller company can be even more critical. Sometimes, those customers are loyal to you, the individual, and not to the company. This is especially true for small service businesses in which the customers can't think about receiving a particular service without thinking about you specifically.

Customer-facing roles are less valuable in product businesses and commodity businesses in which the customers are strict with respect to buying products based on price and not on convenience. However, don't forget that the sales process is still built on relationships, and a savvy salesperson can wield considerable power and influence with the client.

In our digital economy, many customer relationships are built on strategic partnerships and indirect sales channels. For example, some of Salesforce. com's revenue (8.3 billion in 2017) was derived from consulting firms, such as Accenture and Deloitte, and a large ecosystem of smaller cloud systems integrators.

They are not alone in this approach. These strategic partner connections can be equally important to your value and job security after the acquisition, such as through the relationships you have with the contract sales groups, value-added resellers, and other sources of referrals. The reality is that the broader your network is inside and outside the organization, the more will it help you on many levels in your career.

Following an acquisition, these customers and partners face some of the same uncertainties that you are facing. Instead of job security, they might be thinking about "vendor security" and wondering whether they will get the same service at the same price on the same payment terms or whether their SLAs will change.

If your company is providing anything in the customer's supply chain in a "just in time" arrangement, any interruption could result in significant disruption and customer inconvenience on their end, including penalties, brand erosion, and lower stock price. Can you imagine what a mess it would be?

Your strategic partners will be worried about one key issue—revenue. In most cases, contracts cover acquisitions, but even though the legal issues might be resolved, relationships are hugely important in a service economy. Relationships can mean the difference between "seamless" integration and feeling "sluggish" or bogged down.

Remember the acquirer's spreadsheet mentality? That can extend holistically to customers and vendors just as it does to employees.

Just as you have been an advocate for yourself and your team, you may need to be an advocate for customers and strategic partners following an acquisition. As usual, over-communicate and highlight and articulate areas of alignment and value. However, if there are troubled partnerships or pain-in-the-ass vendors, there's no better opportunity to clean up the mess. Done!

Communicating with Clients

Pay special attention to contract renewals following an acquisition. If a renewal is coming up, make sure to "grease the skids" and ensure that there is no lapse in service or availability.

Another contractual area is a Service Level Agreement (SLA). Communicate with your customer and reassure them that everything is in order, and that they will not suffer any lapse in service with the new owner. SLA terms usually survive an acquisition, but a friendly word can help maintain the relationship at the highest level and put any potential concerns at ease. That customer loyalty translates directly to profitability. Loyal customers are the ones who are least likely to switch because of an increase in price.

Similar to SLAs, payment terms can become an issue under the new management. The new company might have a stricter policy with respect to invoices and payment might be expected on a "net 10" versus a "net 30" framework. That switch in payment terms could have a large impact on the cash flow of small customers or of large customers with large invoices.

You should also make the following assessment: Is your customer a desired customer under the new ownership? Would your new owner have pursued your customer previously? Sometimes, you have to help your new owner discard unprofitable or problematic customers, especially the ones that clog up your support centers or sue you at every affront.

You may be in a position of providing reassurance to jittery clients who want to leave because of the new ownership ("I stopped using that bank five years ago, and I came to your bank because the service was much better. Now, I'm back where I started!"). Remind them that because of your presence, that original level of service and quality will remai intact.

Strategic Partners

In most cases, a partnership or sales channel agreement will legally survive the acquisition. Even though this takes care of the legal question, there is no guarantee of continuity and value. If your boss has been let go along with the manager above him or her along with most of your team members, the partnership might not be as viable as before. In such circumstances, the value proposition would have changed.

In the Whale Scenario or Merger of Equals Scenario, the newly combined company may have more capital resources and customers, and your partner might bring less to the table. Your buyer may have a set of superior strategic partnerships already in place. You may not need the partnership any longer. Therefore, it might be in your best interest to fire the partner at the next renewal or begin the timetable on an opt-out clause.

In a Private Equity Scenario, in which your buyer takes your listed public company private, you may have more freedom or more need to pursue strategic partners and joint ventures than before. I've seen this first hand once the Wall Street handcuffs were removed. This is a real opportunity for you to show value to the new owners. **Get excited!**

Vendors

In some companies, an excellent supply chain is the strategic advantage and vendor relationships can be as mission critical as customers and strategic partners.

For example, you might be in the retail grocery business. Your revenue and profit margins are dependent on very strong relationships with food providers, no matter whether they deal in providing bulk goods or fresh produce. When a customer purchases a box of cereal or an avocado, the intelligent automated supply system notifies the store management, the distribution warehouse, and the food provider so that a replacement item is on the shelf within minutes and another replacement moves along from the cereal factory and avocado orchard towards the store in a familiar fashion.

In this model, what the customer experiences are convenience and a guaranteed low price, and every entity in the supply chain makes money from the retail transaction.

After an acquisition, every vendor in the supply chain will need reassurance that the business will proceed as usual with the same operational and quality guidelines, pricing, and payment terms. While that scenario is probably next to impossible, you will have unusual value and importance in all those discussions.

Well done, you!

24

DON'T BE THAT GUY—DEALING WITH YOUR ACQUIRER'S SYSTEMS AND WORKFLOWS

"I failed my way to success."
—Thomas Edison

This book is predominantly about the human element, but this chapter addresses technology, in general, and the technical touchpoints that are in flux because of the acquisition, in particular.

You may have worked for a cash-strapped start-up in bootstrapping mode, and you may not be used to having the capital or cash flow to provide the business basics.

If your founders started the company with personal credit cards, or took out home equity loans, that start-up "siege mode" mentality of austerity (having no money), could linger and remain even when the company has become successful. You may have been operating without the normal business tools that your competitors or counterparts are used to.

You might have been using a modified Excel spreadsheet for your Customer Resource Management (CRM) or, perhaps, a freemium version of a software as a service (SaaS) application, avoiding subscription fees whenever possible. The big enterprise systems are generally overkill for small teams, as you only leverage a fraction of the capabilities.

If you worked for a small nimble company that has been acquired by a large whale, it might be time for you to graduate from using Gmail to Outlook for email, Google Hangouts to WebEx for meetings, and value-added storage services such as Box vs. your personal Dropbox account.

These days, the most difficult transition for my team would be moving from Slack to Microsoft Lync for chat purposes. *Cringe, right?* However, these brands are highly tangible examples of corporate culture in terms of productivity tools. They are entrenched, at least for now, in every large organization that I've seen. Depending on your frame of reference, it may be a hard pivot, but it will help if you can adapt quickly.

Or, you might find out that your smaller company was more technologically savvy in one area or another than your acquirer. Moreover, there may be different regulatory or procurement processes at play that may inhibit productivity.

You might find things bogging you down due to the formality of a larger corporate organization, especially one that is a public company and has to answer to Wall Street and its insatiable hunger for the delivery of quarterly results.

You may have been doing things such as Agile development without actually calling it that. Small companies can be incredibly efficient and productive with respect to developing and shipping new products quickly. On the other hand, larger companies try to mimic this with an assortment of process improvement disciplines and fail more often than not. The reality is that big ships require deep water and considerable time to turn around.

Or, you might run into something such as the Six Sigma in which each project that is carried out within an organization follows a defined sequence of steps and has specific value targets, for example, reduction of process cycle time, pollution, and costs and increasing customer satisfaction and profits.

Tread carefully here, as this landscape is littered with trained agents who are ready to spread the Six Sigma principles at every water cooler discussion. When someone from the new company asks you about being a Black Belt, they are not asking you about your kids' Taekwondo rank. Ha! It's a Six Sigma term and can lead to some interesting conversations if you are not aware.

According to IASSC, a certified **Lean Six Sigma Black Belt™** (ICBB™) is a professional who is well versed in the **Lean Six Sigma Methodology** and who leads complex improvement projects, typically in a full-time capacity.

This is a far cry from the expertise demonstrated by good ol' Mr. Miyagi in *The Karate Kid* movie we all loved. Still want more? Okay, the following are six other Six Sigma terms that get tossed about:

- Defects per Opportunity (DPO)
- Force Field Analysis
- Tollgate
- Value Stream Mapping
- Kaizen
- 6 Ms

However, you insist, "We had a lean organization." Who are these jokers with their new lingo?

Your small, start-up culture might have been out-Six-Sigma-ed by all the Black Belts at the acquirer's company, but it doesn't matter. As painful as it might be, take the class, earn the belts, and learn the lingo, including all the acronyms. **You got this!**

Come out of the other end with a new frame of

reference and use what works for you and your initiatives while going forward. I know I have not presented it in the best light, but there are some solid portions of the framework, IMHO.

Ok, well, if you are not sold on this idea, allow me to elaborate a little . . . Check out the television show *30 Rock* that created a fantastic spoof of a corporate Six Sigma retreat called "Retreat to Move Forward." That episode is so dead-on, you might feel as if you are actually at work. I know you are tempted. ;-)

Another thing you might notice in a larger company is the prevalence of formal meetings, and, at the extreme, a meeting is held to "talk about meetings." You can't make this sh%* up . . . In fact, I know that there is a good portion of you right now with a grin on your face as you know exactly what I am talking about.

These meetings tend to be far more about attendance-taking and "facetime" than about really moving the dial forward. Everything that is discussed (timelines, tasks, and responsibilities) is already present in the online program management system, but, for some reason, certain members of the management believe that employees don't fully grasp a concept or understand something unless it is belabored on a Tuesday morning or worse at 4:30 pm on a Friday.

I hate to admit it, but I've been on both sides of this

over the years. Everyone has a boss, so these things tend to affect the lower ranks the worst. Many smaller companies have "huddles," that is, informal bursts of information sharing, which usually comprise the high points versus an exhaustive "around the horn" polling by each team member.

Scrum check-ins (or any of its half-million variations) for 15-20 minutes every morning is a tried and tested method for developing successful product teams around the globe, so you might want to give it a whirl if you haven't done it before.

To maintain your nimble, entrepreneurial culture in the midst of a formal, hierarchical one, you might want to bring in some outside reading related to your industry or your professional development. When the information is coming from another source, such as from a new bestseller or HBR article, they tend to listen more. It takes time.

However, remember that you must fit into their world as best as you can so trust can start to be established.

Wax on, wax off!

25

DON'T LET THE SYNERGY GET IN YOUR WAY

> "Research shows that the climate of an organization influences an individual's contribution far more than the individual himself."
> —W. Edwards Deming

Isn't it a bit funny that the announcement and press release for almost every acquisition contains the word "synergy." What is up with that?

The word "synergy" is a noun, and it's defined as "the interaction or cooperation of two or more organizations, substances, or other agents to produce a combined effect greater than the sum of their separate effects."[20] You might also see it expressed in the plural form as "synergies," as if the combination of two companies automatically doubles anything by nature of linkage. Doesn't it sound a bit ridiculous when I lay it out in this way?

---

[20] https://en.oxforddictionaries.com/definition/synergy

If you are around long enough and lucky, you might even be graced with the more elusive form of "synergistic." Please observe a moment of silence when it happens. ;-)

Synergy comes in two basic forms (cost savings and increased revenue) and a multitude of flavors.

Merged companies will enjoy shared information technology resources, including shared storage and infrastructure. In addition, they won't need two licenses for HP's data warehouse, SAP's CRM, and Oracle's over-bloated installation at the datacenter.

However, that doesn't mean that it will be easy to converge. One of the biggest challenges that you will face with enterprise software is that, in most situations, it is customized or "slightly hacked" to fit the organization. When the two come together, your customizations are most likely not to align perfectly.

The two companies will benefit from supply chain efficiencies, including discounts from carriers and more marketplace clout for moving goods around the physical world. There will be no more waiting in line at the port in LA or Savannah; moreover, expedited logistics and the optimized distribution centers will be a welcomed change.

Research and Development (R&D) synergy means that the combined firms can boost lagging development with the best practices and the innovation of a more nimble, entrepreneurial company, as it often happens when a large public company acquires a technologically savvy start-up. Cisco was very good at this practice, which was often termed as a "buy vs. build" growth strategy.

Ok, let's take a moment and stop picking on the IT juggernauts and pivot over to life sciences. Do you remember a firm named Valeant Pharmaceuticals? They were flush with cash and had a good run of buying up everyone they could get their hands on.

One company might buy another just for accessing the other companies' patents and trade secrets or they might buy a supplier to create a vertical market alignment.

Synergy can also come about from complementary products, for example, between a company that produces very high-end medical robots for operating rooms and a company that owns a regional hospital chain and who just so happens to be looking to adopt the latest healthcare technology and to reduce the operating costs. I'm getting excited about the possibilities just writing about this fictitious situation... Another synergy you might see is geographical or is tied to industry specialization. Therefore, a European pharmaceutical company might purchase a North American pharma company to increase its global footprint, market dominance, and revenue.

Often, the synergy is industry-related and allows a large company to leapfrog ahead and enter new markets more quickly. Oracle was a traditional leader in enterprise database products and services, mostly, on-premise software. In 2012, Oracle bought the SaaS marketing automation upstart Eloqua for $810 million and instantly entered the arena of cloud computing.

Similarly, Microsoft bought Skype ($8.5B) and LinkedIn ($26B) and Google bought YouTube a decade ago, and YouTube is now one of the primary revenue-driving subsidiaries at Google (Alphabet), a F%@#$%* steal at $1.6B. Take a moment and think about how many individuals out there make their entire living, that is 100% of their income from YouTube today by uploading two or three edited (professionally, at that) vlogs on the platform for their hungry fans.

Most recently, Amazon's $13.7B acquisition of the upscale grocer Whole Foods in 2017 really got people thinking about synergy.

Was Amazon getting deeper into the grocery business? Was it weaponizing against Walmart on their brick and mortar turf? Or, picking up new Amazon Prime customers from Whole Foods' high-end demographic?

Or, did they just want to be able to deliver that deliciously healthy $6 bottle of asparagus water to your house with a drone?

When things sound too good to be true, know that they probably are. I march to the beat of my own drum. I will approach most of the business situations I encounter positively, but I will not tolerate fudging the facts and B.S.

It's fine when the CEO mentions **synergy** at the acquisition press conference, but how do you, as a manager, operationalize it and how do you realize the potential?

Some of the answers are in Chapters 11 and 12 of this book, but much of it goes back to the information provided in Chapters 16, 17, and 18. How do you understand and translate the new culture, how do you take care of the direct reports in your group, and, ultimately, how do you manage that pool of talent that is under your control?

> *"The combined portfolio of leading vertical internet assets will be a powerful one," said Herald Chen, Chairman of Internet Brands, K.K.R. member, and head of the technology industry team. He added, "We look forward to supporting and accelerating the growth and global expansion of the businesses."*

I might print this synergy statement from this 2017 press release and figure that my marching orders hinge on the following formula:

Supported Internet Technology + Accelerated Growth = Global Expansion

Every moment I'm at work, I should be honing my technology skills, looking for growth opportunities in new products, new partners, and new clients, and exploring those efforts on a global scale. I should be asking myself:

- What tasks can I accomplish today that I could not before?
- What resources and firepower do I have at my disposal today?
- Who can I talk with whom I couldn't talk with previously?
- Where can I go on the planet that was previously off-limits to me?
- What limitations are now removed?

I'm not talking about a complete makeover in the Blue-Sky style, but, perhaps, there is a way to map out some small iterative steps along each of the five questions that are listed above.

We might have been a start-up once, that is, a little fish in a little pond, but then we became a bigger fish. But the pond got bigger and so did the other fish. Therefore, not only do we have more resources than we did before, but also greater expectations for making the dealmakers look smart. I still need to do my job in the way in which I've always done it—by exhibiting savviness, being nimble, and demonstrating design thinking with a bit of levity thrown in. That's the part that has not changed during all this upheaval.

26

HELLO, MILWAUKEE! RELOCATION COULD BE THE DEALT HAND

> "We keep moving forward, opening new doors, and doing new things, because we're curious and curiosity keeps leading us down new paths."
> —Walt Disney

There's quite a bit written for the role of HR departments with respect to best practices for relocating employees after an acquisition (for example, selecting employees on merit, defining roles, and establishing communication). However, not much guidance is available if the relocation is happening to you. At least, it is so from my exploration.

There might be an element of "If you want to keep your job, you will have to move to Milwaukee next week." Really?

This impersonal "cog" approach does not speak to your family and community roots, your school and church connections, your core principles, or even your volunteer contributions. You have made a home here and, unless you are single without kids, you will not likely be eager to leave. Moreover, you may be looking after elderly parents or other family members.

However, in the spreadsheet mindset of the acquirer, there is little recognition of the human element or your personal life and priorities. The following are the three ways in which you can look at relocation:

1. You might just be moving to a better community or a larger city with more career and cultural opportunities. Small companies can be formed anywhere, but their acquirers tend to cluster in larger, coastal cities, such as San Francisco, Miami, or New York, in the United States. This is happening currently in St. Louis, where Monsanto (Bayer), Anheuser-Busch (InBev), and Express Scripts (Cigna) have all been acquired and many of the headquarter jobs are moving out of the area.

2. The mandatory transfer might have happened anyway without an acquisition. The previous company might have asked you to move "voluntarily" as a condition of keeping your job. This is pretty normal.

3. The new city might be a better place for you to be working in if things don't work out with the acquirer and you didn't even have to pay for the move!

What you want is a consideration for making this move and for the upheaval and any inconvenience that you might face.

You would need a relocation package or, at the very minimum, reimbursement for all your moving expenses (some of which are tax-deductible in April of the next year; however, this doesn't help you during the moving process). These are all reasonable requests, considering the major life disruption that is knocking on your front door.

Therefore, a strong (perfect world) relocation package can include the following:

- **House Hunting.** A paid trip (all transportation and lodging costs included) to the new city to find a future home that will be suitable for your family. Make sure that your travel meals and airport parking expenses are included as well.
- **Home Buying/Selling.** According to Zillow, the company usually covers costs of selling your home and purchasing a new home, including closing costs, real estate commissions, and other normal expenses.[21]
- **Job Search Assistance for Spouses and Partners** (also known as a "trailing spouse" benefit)

---

[21] https://www.zillow.com/blog/relo-101---what-you-should-know-about-relocation-packages-70147/

- **Transportation.** This includes providing travel expense to the new location.
- **Temporary Housing.** This includes facilitating furnished rental housing or a hotel, including any rental fees and deposits and renter's insurance policy cost.
- **Professional moving expenses (full pack and unpack)** or rental of truck/trailer for self-managed moves.
- **Lump Sum Option.** The company might make an estimate for your relocation and opt to give you a lump sum. You can handle all the relocation arrangements. However, make sure that you get that lump sum upfront. You should not be expected to provide the receipts upfront, but you will be expected to keep up with all your moving receipts.

Negotiating Your Relocation Package

Look for HR cutting corners (for instance, by hiring a cousin with a truck to move you versus a national brand mover) and "wholesale" deals that can be made with movers and realtors based on volume, in cases in which the service level is low and the benefits are dubious.

Before you accept your "relo" package and make arrangements to move, double-check the specifics with HR so that you know exactly what will be covered or reimbursed. You don't want to get stuck with expenses for items that you thought would be covered.

Remember . . .

1. Ask questions
2. Know the exact numbers
3. Get it in writing

In addition, don't feel bad for the company. Everything in your relocation package is a legitimate business expense, and it was probably included in the pricing of the acquisition. The money has already been spent! So, sleep well, my friend!

Moreover, the allocated cost to move you is far cheaper for the company than the cost of recruiting, hiring, and training a new manager.

Watch out for an acquirer who doesn't account for the cost of living differences between your current city and the new city to which you would relocate. Make sure your salary is maintained relatively (while moving from a high-cost region to low-cost region) or enhanced (while moving from a low-cost region to a higher-cost region). Moving from Raleigh, NC to San Francisco, CA is a prime example of that, so be prepared.

Just like everything else in an acquisition, you will need to be your own advocate. Push back (politely and professionally) if something does not seem reasonable.

Now, embrace the new city, venture out to discover all it offers and enjoy the ride!

27

SILVER SEVERANCE, COPPER CUSHION

> "Whoever said money can't buy happiness simply didn't know where to go shopping."
> —Bo Derek

The term "golden parachute" is used to describe any large termination payment that is made to an executive, including a severance payment associated with the change-in-control agreement, and payouts that are given to executives because of an acquisition. The idea here was to motivate CEOs to evaluate potential mergers that might be good for shareholders without making them worried about losing their jobs.

Most golden parachutes go to C-Level executives, but yours might fall into the category of a **"copper cushion," "silver severance package,"** or some compensation that recognizes your value to the company.

What if you are offered a severance package?

First off, celebrate your good fortune. Not everyone gets a parachute or a severance package.

It is imperative that you remain professional. Celebrate your good fortune with your spouse or your Chocolate Lab, but do not discuss it openly at work. Remember, every severance package is different, but almost all flavors have a monetary component. However, there are some people who merely get a month's salary, unpaid vacation, and get escorted to the door by security.

HR will lay all of this out for you, but now is not the time to rejoin the water cooler rumor mill down the hall.

Second, review the offer soberly. You're agreeing to do something that your employer wants from you in exchange for a sum of money if you live up to your side of the bargain. There may even be some kind of non-compete agreement as a part of the offer if you have worked for them for a long time. However, the good news here is that the non-compete clauses in some states can be difficult to enforce.[22]

Unfortunately, you rarely get to negotiate a severance package. You are probably getting Package 11-B, which includes many attractive exit benefits, but you

---

[22] https://www.laboremploymentperspectives.com/2013/01/22/covenants-not-to-compete-yes-they-can-be-enforceable/

definitely will not be getting all of them.

Obviously, if you are still uneasy about the agreement package, it is probably a good idea for you to discuss it further with an employment attorney. If so, check out Avvo.com to find the qualified assistance.

The following are a few things that you need to consider:

- Confirm if the agreement includes reimbursement for any unused paid time off or sick days
- Confirm whether the agreement requires you to waive any claim for unemployment benefits
- Make sure to clarify the availability of insurance (life, health, and dental)

If I were to ask for anything that has been mentioned above and beyond, it would be education money for training in a field or job function that I wanted to move into to make me more marketable later. The other would be insurance, if it is not covered by default.

When it comes to negotiating, certain phrases are gems, whereas others will never sparkle. For example, one gem you might want to ask is, "What kind of flexibility do we have here?" as it relates to the package. There are plenty of others, depending on your situation, so conduct some online research.

Third, get the deal in writing. Never accept a verbal offer. I included this as it can happen with remote employees, so, if that is you, be sure to wait for the email follow-up.

Finally, sit tight. Keep your head down and do your job, remaining secure in the fact that you will have a soft landing eventually. This severance could be your ticket to taking some time off and traveling, spending time with family (walking them to school), or shooting for the fences and actually exploring that start-up idea that you've been nurturing since graduate school.

Make it happen!

28

MIC DROP: THE BAIL-OUT OPTION

"If you can't fly then run, if you can't run then walk, if you can't walk then crawl, but whatever you do you have to keep moving forward."
—Martin Luther King, Jr.

The leaders of acquisition often speak about accomplishing the "seamless integration" of the two companies. This essentially means that the integration doesn't have any negative impacts. Now, the eternal optimist in me loves this! However, in more cases than not, it's only a nice aspirational goal.

Sometimes, the acquisition might not be a good fit for you. However, you should feel content with the knowledge that you gave it your best shot. You went with the flow. You patiently watched as positions were eliminated all around you, sometimes, with no notice at all. You watched as the collaborative and positive culture of your company was consumed by a corporate culture that left little clean air for your ideas or contributions to breathe.

If you have responded to the acquisition positively and optimistically, but are continually "hitting the wall" with the company's management, it, probably, is about them and not you. It might be time for you to move on.

Therefore, you should give yourself the bail-out option.

Seth Godin in *The Dip* calls this "the Strategic Quit."[23] You may not think of yourself as a quitter, but, maybe, it's time for you to learn about the art of quitting. Permit yourself to walk away. It may not feel natural, but it may be necessary.

The following are some definite signs that should lead you to consider a Strategic Quit:

1. You have been left off emails and other business critical communication threads.
2. You are not included in projects in which you are a subject matter expert or have customer/ partner relationships.
3. You are overloaded with projects with unreasonable deadlines and deliverables.
4. You have encountered major project obstacles or outright sabotage.
5. You have not been included in offsite planning meetings and sales kick-off.
6. You have been uninvited from something you've already been invited to join.

---

[23] Godin, Seth, *The Dip*, Penguin Group (2007)

7. You experience "death by a thousand papercuts:" This comprises tiny slights, unreasonable rejection on expense reports, professional dues, or vacation requests, the downgrading of office space (window office to internal office, office to cubicle, cubicle to the broom closet). Keep your red stapler hidden!

8. You are subjected to obvious snubs and overt omissions, especially, when made in a public setting such as a meeting or retreat.

9. You are left out of the bonus plan when you have demonstrated performance.

10. You have to face a negative adjustment/ reduction to the stock option plan

11. You are subjected to unacceptable cultural deviations and behavior, which would not have been acceptable in the previous company.

12. You are not included in the professional conferences that you would have normally attended.

Any single item from the above list might be a deal breaker or it may be a combination of a few of them or a cascade of many items. Alternatively, it may be nothing overt at all and just a series of subtle signals.

You might experience the following "side effects" in your personal life:

- Increased appetite/snacking or loss of appetite
- Insomnia or trouble with getting up in the AM

- General malaise or apathy
- A feeling of dread on Sunday nights
- Strained relationships (on the home front)
- Physical manifestations (pain)
- You are easily distracted or face trouble in finishing easy tasks

Listen to your gut. If things don't feel right, they probably are not.

If you decide to leave, know that you are not giving up. Far from it. You are actually giving yourself a chance to start over somewhere else sooner. Why spend another minute being miserable?

How much longer do you want to carry around this dead weight on your back? It might be better to find a place that is willing to carry you for a while!

Make your own weather!

Therefore, if you do decide to leave, do it with surgical precision. Think about how Dexter would do it . . . I'm just kidding. But, don't leave halfway. Leave and don't look back.

If you are going to have any regrets, you should only regret that you didn't leave sooner. You should have no guilt about this. No one asked your opinion about the acquisition. In addition, they're certainly not asking for your help right now.

As Godin suggests, the buyers/new management might be counting on you to leave. A certain amount of attrition is built into the acquisition plan. Don't waste your perseverance on a company that no longer deserves or values your talents, contributions, and initiative.

Tips for Resigning

1. Do it relatively quickly
2. Do it without emotion (at least limit it if you can)
3. If you have been left out of the communication loop by the new management and your counterpart division, you do not have an opportunity to be communicative. Just be respectful, professional, and considerate.
4. You are not a job hopper! You can easily ascribe your reason for leaving to "acquisition." Remember that most people have experienced a buy-out in their careers. Therefore, most people will understand.
5. Don't burn bridges. While you may need this job as a future reference, if the members of the higher management haven't been supporting you, they may not be a great source as a positive reference. Solicit your peers and your former boss instead.
6. Keep your resignation letter short and sweet— two to four sentences will do.
7. Don't worry about your next opportunity. If you feel like you were making a contribution, and it

wasn't recognized, be confident that another employer in the future will see your value. I'd say you can count on it.

8. Plan your exit. Make a checklist of all the things, such as a final paycheck, accrued sick and vacation days, 401k or pension transfer, that you need to secure before you leave.

Open the door and walk out confidently. Take a deep breath and enjoy the fresh air.

Your next adventure awaits you!

29

INCOMING! PREPARING FOR THE NEXT ACQUISITION (IT'S GONNA HAPPEN)

"There are no secrets to success. It is the result of preparation, hard work, and learning from failure."
—Colin Powell

Look at the stats. Another acquisition will find you, if not in five years, certainly within the next decade. If your current acquirer has bought the company to flip it, it's inevitable.

Let's take a moment and go over just one local example of this that I recently heard about.

Having been founded in 1995, the start-up Accordant Health that is based in Greensboro, NC, was a health maintenance organization (HMO) specializing in complex, chronic diseases. AdvancePCS acquired it in 2002. In 2003, Caremark bought AdvancePCS for $5.3 billion. In 2007, CVS acquired Caremark in a $26.5 billion deal. Healthcare experts and people familiar with Accordant say that the AdvancePCS acquisition of Accordant was the key piece in the Caremark deal that happened a year later.

You might be lucky. You might be in a company that is never bought or, maybe, you are allowed to work for your company's first acquirer indefinitely.

However, if you think another acquisition is a possibility, the following are the 10 things you can do to prepare for next time:

1. Make sure you are working on any project or product or deal that is mission critical to the company

Volunteer for projects and assignments. Hone your project management and public-speaking skills. Seek out "Skunk Works" teams that are involved in new product innovation. The 3M Corporation famously permitted its employees to devote 15% of their time to new areas of development, outside of the normal development channels. Take a lateral job move into a customer-facing role or something in business development or product marketing. Take a non-technical role in a technical area, such as agile DevOps (software development) or user acceptance testing. Socialize with product managers and engineers and sales managers. Get on the revenue side of the business.

2. Take a leadership role in a project, product, or deal

Learn as much as you can from industry conferences. Most of the keynotes and panel proceedings stream online on YouTube or your company's website. Make time for them. Volunteer for having more responsibility for projects and initiatives. Identify allies and executive sponsors who can help you move along. Take a page out of venture capital and create an informal advisory board for yourself. Take smart people out for lunch. Conduct informational interviews. Break out of the pack. Make a lateral job move that puts you in more of a leadership role.

3. Are you in a profit center or cost center?

Volunteer for profit center assignments. Make a lateral move into a profit center (be inspired by Jon's story from 1989—he was an AVP in a bank and head of the bank training department with six direct reports, no customer contact, and minimal budget responsibility. An earnings hiccup and a resignation allowed him to move into managing a retail bank branch with three direct reports, customers, and P&L responsibility). Figure out how to make your cost center an innovation/profit center.

4. Domain and technical expertise (subject matter expert)

Form a personal "advisory board" of subject matter experts. Write blog posts on your technical topic on Medium and repost it on LinkedIn. Write a book or an eBook. The reality is that If you have written 15 or more blogs, then you have enough material for an eBook. Write an introduction and put it up on Kindle. Speak at conferences. Get out there!

5. Functional Expertise

Form an advisory board of functional experts. If you are stranded in a back-office role with little hope of shifting over to a profit center or customer-facing position, become the best accounts payable or human resources manager you can be. Blog about best practices and innovation in your job function. Join the local chapter of a professional association and volunteer. These groups are usually understaffed. You might end up on the board after your first meeting, even if it's as a membership chair or annual event organizer. Leverage your blogs and speak at professional conferences.

6. Develop Your Emotional Intelligence and Interpersonal skills

Read all the books and online content on the topic you can find. Attend personal development workshops or retreats. Take it seriously! Work with a mentor, therapist, or hire a business coach.

7. Sponsors/Advocates

Initiate informational interviews with potential sponsors. Look for projects, work assignments, and social events that will put you in proximity to potential advocates.

8. Sponsors/Advocates (among potential acquirers)

Identify friendly, supportive individuals in the acquiring organization once the dust has settled. Conduct informational interviews and volunteer for work assignments in product development and customer-facing areas. Take advantage of social events. Don't be a wallflower. Get out there and mingle.

9. Develop Industry Relationships (market validation)

Extend your network. Check LinkedIn regularly and stay involved in the conversations. Looking for a tried and true old-school approach, take a colleague or social contact to coffee, lunch or post 5pm libation.

10. Establish and Evolve Customer Relationships

As a key to any good relationship, communication is an essential way to build customer relationships. Ask clients for feedback and show appreciation. And always aim to exceed expectations.

30

WHAT'S YOUR M&A WAR STORY?
(CALL TO ACTION)

> "There is no greater agony than bearing an untold
> story inside you."
> —Maya Angelou

Well, you've heard my M&A story. I've recounted as
much of it as I can recall and added in my wisdom
and guidance. I've woven in tremendous amounts of
common sense and tribal knowledge to help you.

**Now it's your turn—what is your M&A survival
story?**

How is it unique and different?

**What strategies and tactics did you use to
navigate your way through the process?**

**How does your M&A story resonate with what
you've just read?**

C'mon, listen to Maya Angelou and tell your story today!

www.acquired.company/YourStory

Feel free to email me directly at:
acquiredbook@gmail.com *with your story, feedback on the book, or interest in writing a foreword.*

When possible and with your permission, my publisher and I would like to consider including your story in a future edition of this book or in a sequel.

Who knows where the road will take us!

THANK YOU!

THE SURVIVAL FITNESS ANALYSIS
WORKSHEET AND SCORECARD:
THE SURVIVAL FITNESS SCORE ™

This can also be viewed and calculated at:
www.acquired.company/TSFS

	Confidence Area	Fitness Points	Score	Data/ Details
1	**Product/ Project/ Deal/ Mission Critical**	Project - 4 Product - 6 Deal - 8 Mission critical - 10		
2	**Leadership Role**	Supporting role - 4 Deputy role - 6 Primary lead - 8		
3	**Profit Center vs. Cost Center**	Cost center - 3 Profit center - 7 Highly profitable - 9		
4	**Technical or Domain Expertise**	New to industry - 3 Some related experience - 4 Knowledgeable - 5 High expertise - 7 SME - 9		

5	Functional (Role) Expertise	New to the role - 3 Related experience - 4 Knowledgeable - 5 High expertise - 7 Ninja - 9		
6	Emotional Intelligence	Improving interpersonal skills - 3 Acceptable - 5 Solid interpersonal skills - 7 Strong interpersonal skills - 9		
7	Executive Sponsors (Old Company)	My boss is still here - 2 1 exec. sponsor - 4 3 exec. sponsors - 6 Board or C-Level sponsor - 8		
8	Executive Sponsors (New Company)	Identified and met a potential sponsor - 5 1 exec. sponsor - 8 2 exec. sponsors - 10 Board or C-Level sponsor - 12		
9	Customer, Partner, and Vendor Relationships	1 Vendor - 3 3–5 Vendors/Customers - 9 5–10 Customers/Partners - 12 10+ Customers or one of the largest customers - 15		

10	Have you been headhunted recently?	Six months ago - 5		
		A month ago - 7		
		Frequently - 9		
	Survival Fitness Total Score	**Less than 50 points: Red Light** *Update your resume and LinkedIn profile* **50–70 points: Yellow Light** *Step up your efforts* **70+ points: Green Light** *Press on and enjoy the ride!* *Well done!*		

KEY M&A TERMS

Acquisition

When one company buys another company and gains controlling interest. The buyer is known as the Acquirer and the purchased company is known as the Acquiree.

A public company will often purchase a private company using cash or stock. Large public companies purchase smaller public companies in order to gain a competitive advantage. A private company can buy a public company and remove it from the stock market. It is also possible for a private company to buy another private company. On occasion, the acquiring company will only buy the assets of the purchased company, rather than purchasing the entire company (assets and liabilities).

Bottom Line

Also known as "net income" once expenses have been subtracted from revenue.

Capitalization

Also known as "market cap," describing a company's permanent capital, which includes long-term debt and equity.

Clandestine Takeover (or) Creeping Takeover

Masking the ultimate goal of a full acquisition, it's possible to buy up to a 5% stake in a company without notifying the governing stock exchange.

Consolidation

The fusion of two companies in which both the companies lose their identity and form a new company. Shareholders get shares of the new company.

Crown Jewels

High-value corporate assets that attract hostile takeovers by potential acquirers. As a defensive measure, a company will sell these assets or mortgage them to discourage raiders.

Defensive Merger

To avoid a hostile takeover, the vulnerable company will sell shares to another company that does not pose an acquisition threat.

Divestiture

The partial sale of a company to a third party, in exchange for cash or securities, also known as a "spin-off."

Friendly Merger

When a company is willingly consolidated with another company. The opposite of a hostile takeover.

Golden Parachute

A lucrative termination package offered to senior executives of an acquired company, used to accelerate the sale and make room for the acquiring company executives to become senior management. A golden parachute is said to create a "soft landing" and strong financial motivation for current executives to step aside.

Greenmail

In a hostile takeover, a corporate raider will purchase a significant number of shares, which forces the vulnerable company to buy back the stock at a higher-than-market price to avoid the takeover.

Horizontal Merger

A merger of two competing firms, resulting in decreased competition in the market.

Hostile Takeover

When a potential acquirer (also called a raider) attempts to gain controlling interest in a company without the target company's knowledge or inclination to do the deal.

Intangibles

As distinguished from physical assets like land, buildings, equipment, inventory, and cash, intangible assets include goodwill and intellectual property (patents, trademarks).

Joint Venture
A less complicated alternative to a merger. When two companies create a separate company in order to pursue a strategic business objective.

Leveraged Buyout
Acquisition of a company by its senior executives, often known as a management buyout. In order to afford the purchase, the buying group invests a smaller amount of equity and "leverages" the larger amount with long-term debt or bonds. This strategy often leaves the new company with the expense burden of servicing the debt in addition to funding operations.

Merchant Banker
An intermediary that makes the financial arrangements for a merger, and takes a fee out of the final settlement.

Merger
When two companies combine and subsume their respective identities into the new company. The assets and liabilities of both companies are transferred to the new company. Pharmaceutical giant GlaxoSmithKline (GSK) was formed in 2000 from the merger of Glaxo Wellcome and SmithKline Beecham.

Pac-Man Strategy
A defensive move where the vulnerable company targeted for acquisition tries to take over the raider.

Poison Pill
Another defensive strategy to avoid a hostile takeover. The target company might issue additional securities (equity), which dilutes the bidder's shares and discourages acquisition. Or the target company might take on excessive debt to make the balance sheet less attractive to a raider.

Private Equity Firm
A private equity firm provides support in the form of financial backing and management expertise to enable the growth and development of private companies. A private equity firm covers its operating expenses with a negotiated management fee and eventually profits from its investment when the acquired company is sold (often to another private equity firm) or becomes a public company.

Spin-Off
Similar to divestiture, also known as a "de-merger." A spin-off occurs when the parent company creates a separate company as a subsidiary or a free-standing corporate entity. Sometimes the spin-off has a higher value when it exists separately from the parent company.

Takeover
Similar to an acquisition. A takeover is typically more disruptive than a friendly merger, happens faster, and often results in the departure of the board of directors and senior management, replaced by executives and

board members preferred by the new owners.

Tender Offer
When the acquirer pursues a takeover by going around normal channels and makes a buyout offer directly to shareholders of the target company to sell their shares. This is usually done with cash, providing the shareholders with liquidity.

Vertical Merger
A merger between companies in the same industry, but at different stages of production process. In other words, a vertical merger occurs between companies where one buys or sells something from or to the other.

White Knight
When a company is under assault by a hostile raider, a white knight helps out financially so the vulnerable company retains ownership. This might result in a friendly acquisition where the core operations are kept intact and the members of senior management keep their jobs.

FURTHER READING

Bellingham, Richard, *Getting People and Culture Right in Mergers and Acquisitions* (2010)

Berger, Jonah, *Invisible Influence: The Hidden Forces That Shape Behavior* (2016)

Buono, Anthony and Bowditch, James, *The Human Side of Mergers and Acquisitions* (2003)

Catmull, Ed and Wallace, Amy, *Creativity, Inc.: Overcoming the Unseen Forces That Stand in the Way of True Inspiration* (2014)

Coelho, Paulo, *The Alchemist* (2014)

Collins, Jim, *Good to Great: Why Some Companies Make the Leap and Others Don't* (2001)

Duckworth, Angela, *Grit: The Power of Passion and Perseverance* (2016)

Eyal, Nir, *Hooked: How to Build Habit-Forming Products* (2014)

Godin, Seth, *The Dip: When to Quit, When to Stick* (2007)

Godin, Seth, *Tribes: We Need You to Lead Us* (2008)

Goleman, Daniel, *Social Intelligence* (2006)

Grant, Adam, *Originals: How Non-Conformists Move the World* (2017)

Hanson, Rick, *The Buddha's Brain* (2009)

Marks, Mitchell Lee et. al., *"Surviving M&A," Harvard Business Review* (April 2017)

Pressfield, Steven, *The War of Art: Winning the Inner Creative Battle (2012)*

Sandberg, Sheryl, *Option B: Facing Adversity and Building Resilience* (2017)

Sandberg, Sheryl (with Mike Lewis), *When to Jump: If the Job You Have Isn't the Life You Want* (2018)

Scott, Kim, *Radical Candor: Be a Kick-Ass Boss Without Losing Your Humanity* (2017)

Sinek, Simon, *Leaders Eat Last: Why Some Teams Pull Together and Others Don't* (2014)

ABOUT THE AUTHOR

As an artist, technologist, and follower of his own drum beat, this book's author, **Keno Vigil**, has crammed a lifetime of fun and work experience into four decades, and he's just getting started.

He started out behind the bar at a restaurant and now leads a thriving business unit for Medscape (a subsidiary of WebMD), which is the largest online physician ecosystem globally. His group creates the leading physician simulation software that is targeted at educating physicians around the globe on the latest medical knowledge and therapies to ultimately benefit patients.

During the course of his career, Keno has worked for restaurants, a print shop, several bootstrapped tech start-ups, as well as a few multinational publicly-traded firms. Keno spends his weekdays developing the patient simulation technology that replicates physicians' real-world experiences in clinical decision-making. He thrives on solving business problems, developing new products, and even tinkering around in the professional video studio that he helped build in North Carolina's Research Triangle Park.

In just two decades, he has experienced six acquisitions (three small and three big), which doesn't make him a global M&A aficionado, but the scar tissue that he has developed from those have sprouted countless "aha" moments.

On a personal level, he enjoys spending time with his family, traveling to unique destinations to experience the food and culture, mountain biking, tackling weekend warrior home projects, and dabbling with various therapeutic art projects (woodworking, painting, and most recently sculpture). He is always eager to experience a new museum or stumble across modern architecture on a walk. The works of painters, Franz Kline and the Belgium wonder, René Magritte, are but a few of his faves. From his father being an artist to his grandfather being a master woodworking craftsman, he has always had this innate desire to work with his hands and create (physical and digital).

Keno believes that curiosity, laughter, and the relentless persistence to find joy in whatever you are working on is critically important, both personally and professionally.

He is not only a fan of stand-up comedians, such as George Carlin, Richard Pryor, and Jerry Seinfeld, but also admires the dry Midwestern delivery of David Letterman.

Finally, he aspires to make a stand-up comedy stint his new side hustle, playing to a packed house on three different continents. Keep an eye out!

Until Next Time!